Praise for

THE
HEALER
OF
SHATTERED
HEARTS

PENGUIN BOOKS

THE HEALER OF SHATTERED HEARTS

A graduate of the University of Pennsylvania, where he was an "ardent atheist," and of the University of Judaism, David J. Wolpe was ordained as a Conservative Rabbi by The Jewish Theological Seminary in 1987. Rabbi Wolpe, who has also studied at the University of Edinburgh and Hebrew University in Jerusalem, is the director of the Ostrow Library at the University of Judaism, which houses one of the largest Judaica collections in the country. He is also the editor of Midrash for the Conservative movement's Torah commentary, which is now in progress.

THE
HEALER
OF
SHATTERED
HEARTS

A Jewish View
of God

DAVID J. WOLPE

PENGUIN BOOKS

PENGUIN BOOKS
Published by the Penguin Group
Penguin Books USA Inc.,
375 Hudson Street, New York, New York 10014, U.S.A.
Penguin Books Ltd, 27 Wrights Lane, London W8 5TZ, England
Penguin Books Australia Ltd, Ringwood, Victoria, Australia
Penguin Books Canada Ltd, 10 Alcorn Avenue,
Toronto, Ontario, Canada M4V 3B2
Penguin Books (N.Z.) Ltd, 182–190 Wairau Road,
Auckland 10, New Zealand

Penguin Books Ltd, Registered Offices:
Harmondsworth, Middlesex, England

First published in the United States of America
by Henry Holt and Company, Inc., 1990
Reprinted by arrangement with Henry Holt and Company, Inc.
Published in Penguin Books 1991

5   7   9   10   8   6   4

Translations of biblical material are from the
New Jewish Publication Society Bible, *Tanakh* (1985),
except where a difference of emphasis or nuance
necessitated another translation. All translations
of Rabbinic materials are the author's own.

THE LIBRARY OF CONGRESS HAS CATALOGUED THE HARDCOVER AS FOLLOWS:
Wolpe, David J.
The healer of shattered hearts : a Jewish view of God /
by David J. Wolpe.—1st ed.
p.   cm.
Bibliography: p.
Includes index.
ISBN 0-8050-1211-7 (hc.)
ISBN 0 14 01.4795 0 (pbk.)
1. God (Judaism)   I. Title.
BM610.W64   1990
296.3'11—dc20   89–35467

Printed in the United States of America

The Lord rebuilds Jerusalem;
He gathers in the exiles of Israel.
He heals their shattered hearts
And binds up their wounds.
　　　　　—Psalms 147:2–3

Contents

Acknowledgments

This book was written while I was a Finkelstein Fellow at the University of Judaism in Los Angeles. The University of Judaism is a supportive, stimulating, and welcoming place, and I would like to thank the faculty and staff, who were an unfailing source of support. In particular, I am grateful to my teacher, Dr. Elieser Slomovic, who first introduced me to the rich delights of Midrash and upon whose erudition I continue eagerly to draw. Mimi Sells gave the proofs a careful and helpful review. Francine and Myles Weiss and friends from Sinai Temple supported and fostered this work, and I appreciate their efforts. I owe a debt as well to Sam Mitnick and to my editor, Marian Wood.

I was fortunate to grow up in a home where love was as freely given as were ideas and encouragement. My deepest thanks to Steve, Paul, Valerie, and Danny. Paul read the manuscript with great care, using his acumen to keep me on track, and his brotherly knowledge to keep me honest. Finally, thanks to Naomi, who contributed to this book in so many ways.

Preface

Samuel Johnson once dismissed a book with the withering comment that it was both good and original, but that which was good in it was not original, and that which was original was not good. Many readers will discover, no doubt, that that which is good in this book is not original. I hope that is the case, because in each generation long-known truths and ideas must be summarized, restated, taken from the great teachers of the past and repeated. Judaism venerates memory, and even in the text of its most noted prayer counsels that all teaching must be accompanied by constant repetition, constant relearning.

What follows is an exploration of some Rabbinic traditions, particularly Midrash, Rabbinic legend, which gives poetic expression to the spiritual fervor of the Jewish people. The legends bequeathed to us by the Rabbis, living some eighteen hundred years ago, can be puzzling to the modern reader, despite efforts made in our time to evaluate, catalog, and clarify much of the material. What is before you is not a history or a work of Rabbinic scholarship. It is an attempt to present some striking images from the tradition, images that may initially seem alien, and suggest that they speak to our lives and situations in often unexpected ways.

The range of the Midrash is wide both stylistically and substantively, but underneath insight, axiom, parable, and fable is a struggle to understand God. In an age when the idea of God is to many doubtful and problematic, the Rabbis deserve our time and attention. Sometimes in the timbre of ancient voices we hear the tones of forgotten truth and are reminded of lost perspectives. In the marvelous play of the Midrash, its delightful ingenuity and deep religious purpose, is much of the spiritual patrimony of the Jewish people.

The intellectual and spiritual debts this book owes to the works of others are too numerous to mention, but it should be said that a great deal is the product of my reading of Martin Buber and, particularly, of Abraham Joshua Heschel. Both of these thinkers, although quite different in many ways, were concerned with the modern relationship to God, and both felt that the relationship must be intimate and immediate. Both spoke as poets as well as philosophers and scholars. I am not suggesting that their views are fully represented by this book; but a reader who wishes to be edified and uplifted can do no better than to turn to each of these sages for his meditations on this world, our place in it, and our relationship to God.

THE
HEALER
OF
SHATTERED
HEARTS

Sources and Shapes
of Faith Today

> Would that I knew how to reach God, how to get to His
> dwelling place. . . . But if I go East—God is not there;
> West—I still do not perceive Him.
>
> —Job 23:3, 8

The Talmudic sage Rabbi Jose, son of Rabbi Hanina, once
told of two miracles. The first was the miracle of the manna.
When God provided the Israelites with manna in the desert,
said Rabbi Jose, the manna assumed whatever shape and taste
they desired: to infants it seemed like mother's milk; to the
young it was succulent, and to the old reviving. On a grander
scale, continued Rabbi Jose, was the miracle of God's word.
When God revealed Himself to the Children of Israel in the
desert, each individual standing at the base of Mount Sinai
heard God's words as a personal and unique address. A public
message to a people was also a private message to each person.
All who stood expectantly at the foot of that arid mountain
understood the meaning of revelation in accordance with their
own striving, their own capacities, their own heart (Pes. de-
R.K. 12:25).*

* Material in parentheses refers to biblical or Rabbinic sources; sources that are
abbreviated in the text appear in full on pages 175–76. Material in brackets is my
explanation to clarify a statement. *Rabbinic* in this book refers to the Rabbis of the
Talmud and Midrash, whose dates are approximately 100 B.C.E. to 600 C.E. Many
of the *Midrashim* (the Hebrew plural of Midrash) were not collected and edited,
however, until much later.

Rabbi Jose's comment invites us to imagine a voice and a message as diverse as humanity. To the zealous, God fashioned each utterance like a resolute call, in the clipped and urgent tones of command. To the reflective, God calmed His voice, and in a softer, slower cadence urged words of thoughtful devotion. For those who understood revelation with their minds, God presented an intricate puzzle, teeming with intriguing variations and possibilities. For those who sought to understand with their hearts, God spoke words of passion, presenting revelation not as insight, but as intensity. To some, God's voice was shattering; to others, soothing. To some a tornado; to others, a tranquil wind. All at once, in infinite echoes, the sound of God's spirit filled every unique, yearning soul.

Each person heard the God that he or she could understand, could embrace, could love. Rabbi Jose offers us a picture of tenderness and Divine regard at this moment of revelation, this moment when, Jewish tradition teaches, heaven was wedded to earth.

We can admire the imagery, but do we share the faith? Although we are all of these things: eager and reflective, analytical and passionate, calm and confused, there is one great difference between us and our ancestors—we do not hear the voice.

There was a time in life when we felt confident of dialogue with God. As children we expected to be favored with a sacred sign; perhaps as a whisper at night, or in some miraculous act in the blaze of midday, God would present Himself to us. To a child, the mundane is a spectacle, and the everyday an amazement. When all the world is wonder, why should not the Author of all these marvels sweep in to bow before us? Yet in time, God's silence and life's disappointments combine to give us the adult conviction that we cannot hear the voice, if indeed there is, in this enormous echoing world, a voice to be heard.

Yet what is difficult to hear in our lives can now and then be heard through history, through the lives and teachings of others. Although God does not speak as we might wish, the hope of guidance is too important, and the implications too immense, to leave the question unexplored. So people still search, still seek traditions that may have preserved something of that miraculous time when humanity was confident that it heard the strains of a Divine message, soft or thunderous, that each could understand.

To begin our own search let us look briefly at the place God has traditionally occupied in Judaism and how that place changed in modern times. For the conflicts and solutions of Judaism are expressions of the confusions of the age, and the lessons we can draw go far beyond one people or one time. A tradition, like the God it honors, speaks with many voices.

INTERNAL STRUGGLES

Judaism without God was unthinkable to an earlier age. Through all the meetings and estrangements of history, in every medium the Jew understood—text, life, and land— God was assigned a role. In joy He was praised; in agony, blamed or supplicated. Jewish imagination was tethered to the certainty of Divinity, and however far it whirled in intoxicated intellectual daring, the central conviction remained: Behind and beyond lived life was its unseen foundation, the single Being who knit the earth and fashioned the firmament, lawgiver and deliverer.

This seamless view of Judaism and God has been unspun by the critiques of our age. Questions of whether Judaism can stand without the God-Idea and attempts to redefine God in impersonal terms are part of a general struggle to understand anew the nature of Judaism. Is it a religion? Is it a people, a nationhood, a civilization? If Judaism is something more than a religion, can God be erased or ignored? Suspending definitional entanglements, we may simply ask: How central is God to Judaism?

Many modern Jews will give God an obligatory nod but insist that the centrality of Judaism lies elsewhere. Conceding that God was at one time the fulcrum of Judaism, they maintain that in our day the balance has shifted. Now the people of Israel are the true focus of Judaism. Perhaps the land of Israel, revived by historical legerdemain and massive sacrifice, is the new "true" meaning. The unsettled and remarkable history of Judaism—that is the centrality of which they speak. God is not central because, we are told in those hard dichotomies so beloved of people who come out on the right side, Judaism is a religion of action, not belief, centered in this world, not standing with its head thrust in clouds that, for all their loveliness, do obscure vision.

This hardheaded realism, which is presumed to characterize Judaism, exempts it from the fuzzy reign of speculative theology. You need not theorize about the nature of thermodynamics to drive a car. While God is acknowledged as part of the redoubtable triad—God, Torah, and Israel—some are convinced that one leg can be removed and still the structure, in a neat twist of metaphysical carpentry, stays standing.

Characterizations of Judaism that preserve it as an essentially modern, enlightened faith have obvious advantages. No sacrifice of currently cherished opinion is required, because Judaism will fit snugly into a niche in modern liberality, the slot marked "polite faith." Jews take great pride, often justly so, in a tradition that places so profound an emphasis on one's actions in this world, on life divorced from any specific belief. "It is only what you *do* that counts" is an attractive assertion. In a world that cries for concrete effort, a religion in which the summum bonum, the greatest good, is to practice justice and mercy seems a perfect fit. This is the position of many of Judaism's most enlightened adherents.

Judaism is richer, however, than either its detractors or some of its adherents acknowledge. It is both this-worldly and otherworldly. To work for good in this earthly realm has always been a prime counsel of Judaism, but never its solitary concern. Jewish visionaries have seen the stars as surely as they have surveyed the land. The same Rabbi who said that one hour of repentance and good deeds in this world is worth more than life eternal also contended that this world is just a hallway leading to the world to come (Pirke Avoth 4:21–22).

The presentation of Judaism as a purely naturalistic culture, divorced from all faith assertions and transcendence, is a disservice to the richness of its history and the encompassing sublimity of its beliefs. During the last century a great deal of effort was devoted to portraying Judaism as unremittingly rationalistic. Scholars sought to prove that Judaism is a perfectly sensible, enlightened system of belief. Anything that seemed murky or superstitious was labeled a tangent, not part of the normative tradition. Gershom Scholem, the great scholar of Jewish mysticism, was introduced to his subject in a meeting with an enlightened Rabbi who had a library of mystical texts. Scholem ingenuously asked him what the books were like. "They are ludicrous," exclaimed the Rabbi. "Do you think I would waste my time reading this junk?" Scholem decided that if the Rabbi could evaluate the texts so definitively without having read them, someone who would actually *read* the material could make quite a mark in the field.

Much Jewish scholarship of our century has been devoted to exploding just such ideational bias, exposing the one-sided constructions of past generations of scholars, particularly those who would ignore all the less lucid and logical sides of Jewish tradition. Myth, mysticism, and Midrash have their place too. Judaism is not a faith composed of modern views piled atop each other with the precision of geometrical theorems to which any modern, reasonable person may calmly affix his or her name. To be fair to the past we must understand all of it, even if sometimes it makes us queasy, and we feel reluctant to claim it as our own.

There are, and have always been, many varieties of Judaism. Understandably, in each age Jews have fashioned the faith to conform to their worldview. But that does not mean that Judaism is infinitely malleable; it cannot change forever and keep its shape. Certain beliefs cannot be added or discarded without radically transforming the structure of the faith.

Through all its manifestations, in every age up to our own day, Judaism has had the idea of God at its heart. Readers of the first sentence of the Bible notice that God is not demonstrated or discussed. His existence is taken for granted: "In the beginning God created . . ." What has animated the Jewish quest in its various forms throughout its history is that greatest conceptual gift given to the world—monotheism.

God is central to Judaism in a way that argument or embarrassment (in this case closely allied) cannot alter. If we are uncomfortable with God, or rejecting, we must at least realize that we reject a central column of Judaism. Belief in God may violate our reason, our sensitivities, even our understanding of justice and goodness; if so, let us at least understand how much of the Jewish tradition is thereby lost.

MODERN SPRINGS OF FAITH

God is at the heart of the Jewish message to the world, and to each individual. There are many ways of understanding that message. But faith is not philosophy, and the particular understanding of God is less critical than the act of acceptance. Philosophy can smooth the crags of coarser belief, refine it, but faith springs from deep in the soul, the inaccessible point where individual conscience touches upon what is larger than itself and apprehends its place and purpose.

Belief is neither anti-intellectual nor antirational. As Rav Kook, the great twentieth-century Rabbi and mystic, once said, "If a person spurns reason, his faith will be full of distortion and falsehood." Faith cannot evade reason, for it involves all of one's being, both reason and feeling wound tightly together inside of us. Nor is faith a blissful confident leap into the comfort of a "supreme protector." As we shall see in what follows, it springs from the night as well as the day. Belief without elements of terror and doubt is fairy tale, not faith.

The aim of this book is not to convince another into faith. Argument alone, as frustrated preachers of all ages learn, is hardly sufficient to revolutionize a life or transmit a faith. *Emunah,* a combination of trust and belief, is viewed by the Jewish tradition as something that one gradually apprehends by plunging into the world with eyes open, by participation in the life of study and the study of life. The aim in what follows is to present an idea, an image of the faith of the Rabbis, and to explore how this can be translated in our own time. These pages are filled, to be sure, with argument, advocacy; there is no reason for reticence in presenting this ancient and wisdom-rich vein in the mine of human history. Still, a decent sense of reality advises a more modest goal than persuasion—shared enthusiasm. With the promptings of Jewish thinkers, ancient and modern, we will try to unfurl a vision of God rooted in a sense of encounter and wonder, of responsibility and beauty.

Belief need not be unsophisticated or simpleminded. The metaphor for faith in religious writing is opening one's eyes—not shutting them tight. To the extent that faith ignores the world, or filters out uncomfortable bits, it is weakened and impoverished. The renowned physicist I. I. Rabi was once asked to name the most significant intellectual influence in his life. The interviewer expected to hear "Einstein" or perhaps "Newton." "My mother," Rabi replied instantly. For each day, he explained, when he would come home from *cheder,* Jewish religious school, his pious mother would say to him, "So Isaac, did you ask any good questions today?" From her, said Rabi, he learned that the key to wisdom is to ask good questions. Like so many of her contemporaries, this woman, growing up in an Eastern European ghetto, had imbibed a great principle of Jewish thought: All things must be weighed, scrutinized, evaluated. Judaism preaches an emunah beset by doubt and ringed round with questions. To believe in God is not to abandon one's mind, and to trust God is not to ignore the deepest misgivings of a troubled heart.

Ultimately, we want to touch what God means in the most pained and private chambers of the human soul. Where anguish is greatest, the religious message is most significant. If God does not speak to suffering, to the shattered hearts of the Psalmist's plea, then He must remain peripheral to our lives. That which does not touch my pain leaves me as I was. Even joy lasts and changes us only when it deepens our understanding and endurance of the pain that is part of living in an unredeemed world.

God must be interpreted anew in each age, and yet remains the same. That is why all theology leans so heavily on the enormous collective thought and writing that has preceded it. Still, novel difficulties arise, for which we should be grateful, as new answers rarely appear in the absence of new questions.

From the beginning of Jewish history, references to God have been almost exclusively male. Although God does not have sexual attributes, it cannot be denied that the constant repetition of male referents has an effect upon the way in which God has been viewed. Judaism, with its exalted estimation of the import of words, cannot ignore their effect, intended or not. This is a problem that has only recently begun to receive the attention it demands, and it poses great difficulties for discussion about God.

We do not yet have an adequate alternative to the "He" that traditionally served as a "neuter" pronoun. For now, we have only expressions of regret at the lack. It is important to realize, since the incidence of references to God as "He" are numerous in the following pages, that it *should* jar on the attentive ear. We should be aware that this word is now a way station to the search for something better. Language influences concepts, and doubtless the roles that a God plays in human life that are traditionally associated with the feminine will be enhanced in our conception, to the richness of religious thought and experience, when we can sort out these newly posed linguistic dilemmas and the underlying conceptual unfairness they often reflect.

The issue of language is but one new condition faced in our day. The untiring refrain of sages throughout time is "We are living in a different age." Yet the millennial upheavals of ancient times did not change the world as rapidly as the frightening whir of invention and revolution that seems a daily accompaniment of contemporary life. Unimaginable changes, which once took hold with the stately pace of generations and centuries, are now the accompaniment of a single lifetime, even a single decade. The world moves so rapidly that understanding, like the trailing runner in Zeno's famous paradox, can never catch up with progress. As soon as we know where we are, we have moved. Analysis suffers from lag time; the very act of summing up is a quixotic gesture on the order of evaluating a single frame while the movie is running. In so fluid a world, we crave stability even as we applaud and encourage change.

One of the traditional designations for God is "rock," and the simple solidity of that term is another indication of why God can prove critical to our thought. The firm grounding of human culture has given way to the enormous speed of human innovation and change. We require some permanence. If all about us must change, we might at least count on the eternity, the immutability of God. For every other constant proposed by the hopeful human brain, from ideas to nations to the earth itself, has proved discouragingly susceptible to change, and even to destruction.

The surge of societal change witnessed in the last two hundred or so years has led, unsurprisingly, to a freakish development in its modern human offspring. Technological capacities grow all out of proportion to the maturity of our moral and aesthetic judgment. The unbalanced hybrid creates an understandable hysteria about what we will do to ourselves. There is no calm; there cannot be. Explosive forces in this world are too powerful and their tension too insistent for tranquillity. We are the first generation to truly understand why the mark of Cain had to be placed on his forehead. From there, destruction ultimately grows: it is from unkempt, wild reason that we destroy, through powers of mind unfettered by conscience or obligation.

We are not less good or caring than those who went before us. But if we are not better, we are doomed. The curse of this generation is that human flaws are magnified, striding in steps inconceivable in any previous age. The fury of a tyrant can slaughter not just his family and rivals, but an entire people. A vaccine can save the world from the ravages of a fatal disease. We live large. There is a Rabbinic legend that the eyes of the righteous can see from one end of the world to the other. Sometimes, the Midrash adds, the sight brings joy, at other times pain (Sifre Num. Pinchas, 136). We *do* see from one end of the world to the other. The sight brings pain, or should. No people before have been granted so resolute a pageant of suffering, hunger, deprivation as we witness each evening. Our electronic eye embraces the whole globe, a miracle of which the Midrashist could only have dreamed. But the enormity of the achievement does not seem to make us righteous.

Onto the stage at this improbable point in history strides a renewal of religion. Piety, often of the most extreme and heedless kind, springs thick and stout across the globe. Those outside of this heated world look on with a puzzled distaste. It once appeared that humanity was moving beyond such atavistic devotion and that religion, if it remained at all, would at least keep a certain civility.

It is hard to be sedate, however, while searching for footing at the fringes of an abyss, and those who feel as though we are at the edge of history will not consider sedate conduct a priority. The canons of civilization are fragile things, and in a time when all of life is imperiled, proper form will seem to many a useless mockery. Commenting on Pharaoh's dream in the Bible in which seven gaunt, lean cows eat seven fat, healthy cows, the Rabbis see an allegory for how people will behave in times of desperation—they will devour one another (M. HaG. 41:3). Elegance is prized, moderation venerated, only when the fundamentals of life are more or less secure. To many in this world, the looming horrors of the modern age validate a return to a fervent, often blind religiosity that takes little comfort from a civilization that has brought us to the brink of annihilation.

So religion has been gifted with renewed fervor by the very scientific mind-set that first weakened its hold on humanity. Science has pressed the question to the center of human consciousness: Are we wise enough to avoid obliterating ourselves? The prospect of cataclysm is a tonic to systems that ask ultimate questions. For science alone will not answer for its own uses. Superlative in the "how," science is helpless with the "why." Or in the case of destruction, the "why not."

This terror has reawakened interest in aspects and options of religion that had lain dormant among modern Jews. Throughout the middle of our century, a hardy rationalism seized those who thought about God; to poeticize about what should rightly be a philosophically purified concept was to lack sophistication. God demanded reason, not rhapsody. This holdover from European rationalism, augmented by certain trends in American philosophy, is gradually giving way. Unalloyed reason disappointed early expectations. Fear has shaken loose some certainties. Answers that sound logical, thought systems that hold together, will not save. You cannot build a meaning for life, a drive to rescue the world, out of the dry theorems of rationalist equations. Once again, people are searching unabashedly for the poetry of faith.

THE POETRY OF FAITH

"Poetry," "mystery"—all the evocative terms that have reappeared in the theological writing of our time have their source and ultimate end in God. Divinity lends sacredness to the mundane order and fills the commonplace with holiness. The poetry of faith consists in spinning out the implications and nature of God in this world, in searching for the mediated reflection of presence. There is no escaping the centrality of God to the religious quest. The Jew who searches for his or her ancestors, wishes to appreciate and learn from their faith, will find the name and numinous sense of God at every turn.

Creation, revelation, and redemption are the three pivotal aspects of human history in the Jewish schema, and all were traditionally ascribed to God. God made the world, revealed His will to humanity, and promised ultimate redemption. Each act, although undertaken by God, was for the benefit of human beings, and humanity has a share in all three tasks: in creating the world, in revealing God's will, and in ushering in redemption.

The human quest, wherever and however defined in Jewish thought, is a joint quest, with humanity and God participating together. So the Midrash interprets the verse that Israel sang upon emerging from Egypt and crossing the sea as an affirmation of partnership. By switching two letters, the verse "This is my God and I will exalt Him" can be made to read "This is my God; He and I . . . ," insisting on an alliance in which human beings and God together seek salvation (Mechilta, Shira). For even God, in the Midrashist's bold reading, cannot seek salvation alone. Thus Rabbi Abbahu's prayer, quoting God's own declaration in the Psalms, claims that God needs Rabbi Abbahu just as Rabbi Abbahu needs God: "Lord of the universe, You have said, 'I am with him in distress.' If You too suffer, save Yourself. By heeding my prayers and pleas for redemption, bring about Your own salvation" (Tanh. B. Acharay 18). God must be prodded by the prayers of human beings to effect His own salvation! If God cannot seek salvation alone, surely human beings cannot.

The lesson is both ennobling and humbling. It touches upon the heart of the Jewish conception of God. On the one hand, following Rabbi Abbahu, God is dependent upon human beings for influence in this world. Divine reliance is an ancient teaching of Judaism. Strange as it may sound at first, God needs the efforts of humanity in His quest for the moral perfection of the world and especially for the dissemination of His name and ways. The Rabbis picture God actually thanking the patriarch Abraham for making Him (God) King of the earth—for without Abraham's active proselytization, God would have remained unknown (Sifre Deut. 313). Not until Abraham served as a sort of Divine advance man was God able to bring His word to the world. That is the summit of human hubris, and yet it is sanctioned by the tradition: We are of concern to God, and He depends upon us for the execution of His will in the world. More, He cares simply for our presence: "When God was alone in the universe [before creating human beings], He yearned for the company of His creations" (Num. R. 13:6). In the catalog of reasons given for the creation of the world, this is in some ways the most touching: God was lonely.

Yet it is humbling to recognize the extent to which the tradition insists we require God's help and guidance. We are constantly reminded that our vaunted power is nothing beside that of the Creator of the universe. Our world is small, and we are in many ways ill-equipped to manage its maintenance. That is our weakness. Our struggles here will not go unaided if we are willing to turn inward and outward and find help. That is our strength.

The history of this bloody century teaches that we cannot escape the obligation to commit ourselves in relation to others and to the world. Indifference is a position as surely as passionate devotion. As the world shrinks, the importance of our stance grows. Each action ripples through the tightly wound human community. There is an inescapable moral and emotional impact to our most mundane deeds. The words of an advertisement to help foster children reads: "You can help, or you can turn the page," rendering the simple act of turning a magazine page into a moral declaration. On what do you spend your money, time, energy? What values do you transmit?

Preoccupation with such questions is indispensable but can also be paralyzing. An uncoarsened sensibility is too vulnerable to survive in a world that can be so unkind. It would be easy, if we truly absorbed the abominations that daily occur, to destroy our resolve, our character, our hope. A certain amount of toughening is needed, a human carapace to ward off the constant assault on caring. Although the Bible teaches "Love your neighbor as yourself" (Lev. 19:18), commentators have long insisted that taking such a command literally would incapacitate us. As the Jewish philosopher Moses Mendelssohn notes, we would have to grieve for everyone's losses as we do for our own. In a world of so much suffering, this would be unbearable. We must care deeply, but not without boundaries.

Such a tidy declaration is only the beginning. How many moral questions can we ask and still live our lives? At what point does a healthy defense become an insensitivity to the needs of others? We know that savagery, inhumanity, and pain lace the world, and it is impossible to address it all. The world is too complex for an easy solution—sensitivity alone is insufficient. We need guidance.

The combination of personal and corporate counsel we seek can come only from God, a God both sovereign in the universe *and occupied with each individual person*. A personal and universal God, whose majesty is tempered by familiarity, is the idea this book explores.

The God of the Rabbis provides the framework for the search, for it is in Rabbinic Midrash that a personal God is most elaborately and beautifully expressed. Unconstricted by the need to formulate law or normative standards, in the Midrash the Rabbis permit themselves to act as fabulists, spinners of folktales, authors of personal and historical dramas. We will hear the intimacy of their poetic images and the plaintive tones of their laments. The constant repetitions and incantations of the ages have not worn the sheen from these vital depictions of God nor dulled the marvelous closeness they bespeak.

The examination of Rabbinic ideas is not a task of archaeology; we are not seeking the past to examine it as a collector would a curio, to admire its antiquarian image and consign it to a dusty display case. The Rabbinic ideas of God speak eloquently even today, offering avenues where we, too, can vitalize our spiritual lives. There is nothing unusual, and certainly nothing new, about this quest. For thousands of years Jews have been engaged in just such energizing explorations. The path has been cleared for us as well. Judaism does not hide its riches, and to learn from it requires only what Solomon asked of God so long ago, a request deservedly earning him a reputation for wisdom—a "listening heart."

POETRY AND THEOLOGY

How literal is the language of faith? Although the Bible and the Rabbis speak quite explicitly of God's feelings, do we truly mean that God gets angry, sad, repentant? The implications of this anthropomorphic language have taken up many volumes in the history of religious thought. For now we will leave the debate to the theologians and philosophers of religion. We are searching for the living language of faith, which can move and inspire, liberate our sense of God and the world, bring us closer to the spiritual center of our lives. It is a matter for later reflection and discussion precisely how these terms, so fraught with emotion, work in a theological context.

In these pages, when we speak of the personality of God, it is a relational not a literal statement. What follows aims to open a door to relationship with God. We will not quell all doubts or solve all the intellectual and theological dilemmas that accompany such a relationship. A relationship begins in the sense of another being, a feel for his or her presence and qualities, and does not rely on specific definable attributes. Definitions are important if one is describing another to a third party (which is, after all, the task of the theologian—to describe God to the reader) but not in order to intimate and conjure for oneself the qualities of a friend. Images culled from the tradition, however imprecise, can enable us to begin feeling our way toward God, a process no less important and certainly not less lasting than the cognitive paths hewn out by systematic thinkers. Could any dispassionate description explain what it is like to be seized by a consciousness of God as vividly as does Jeremiah: "I thought, I will not mention the Lord. No more will I speak in His name. But His word was like a raging fire in my heart, shut up in my bones. I tried to hold it in, but I could not. I was helpless" (20:9)? At times the story, the quotation, the question is more eloquent than volumes of argument.

It is easy to conclude that the Jewish tradition is concerned not with images but with action. Judaism places great emphasis upon the performance of the proper action in the designated time and manner. The necessity of appropriate action leads to an enormous preoccupation with the details of the action itself. At times it appears that what one is told to do is suspended alone, without rationale, without even the warmth of theological covering. This is an understandable but grievous misperception. Behind each action prescribed by the Jewish tradition lies a treasury of images, speculation, and feelings, which find earliest expression in the writings of the Bible, the first preserve of tradition. Permitting these images to capture us, delight and move us, appeal to our fancy and intellect is a great liberation of the spirit. Let us accomplish that receptivity before we undertake the necessary systematization. Anatomy is indispensable, but one should first be able to recognize a person.

That is why no attempt at extended argument follows.

The classic texts of Jewish tradition, the Bible and the Talmud, point the stylistic way for one who wishes to write about God. Neither is a philosophical treatise. Indeed, it has been pointed out that not a single technical philosophical term appears in all of Rabbinic literature!* The language is of law, of storytelling, of poetry, of parable, of homily—all the richness of the experienced world, all of it suggesting the Divine presence.

IDOLS OF THE AGE

"God has no heir," said the Zionist thinker Jacob Klatzkin, reformulating the oft-expressed thought about the "death" of God. If God is gone, there is no substitute, no other being or concept that can take the place of the traditional Deity. What is true for a society is equally true for the individual. "You shall have no other gods before Me," the second commandment, embodies a psychological truth as well as a Divine injunction. Anything else human beings raise to the level of God, whether it be money, fame, achievement, or even other people, is a species of idolatry and doomed to fail.

Idolatry in our age, however veiled, always distills to the worship of human beings. It may be the worship of the products of their hands, such as art; or the worship of human power, as manifested in money or in political position. A tragedy of humanity in our time is the certainty that what we see is what alone exists, what we create is alone worthy; that by virtue of an existence whose origins we do not understand and whose beauty we did nothing to merit, we are all that is worthwhile. We suffer the peculiar blindness of those who see only the visible.

* Harry A. Wolfson, *Philo* (Cambridge, Mass.: Harvard University Press, 1947), 1:92.

The emptiness of those ideals resounds in the hollows of our selves. We are not happy, and so we turn to those who will make us happy. But happiness is a by-product, not an aim. You cannot be made happy, paradoxically, by pursuing happiness alone. Perhaps you can be comfortable, even satisfied; but happiness, deep contentment of soul, can arise only from the pursuit of something greater, a sense of life well lived. Happiness itself is elusive, and, moreover, contentment is hardly the highest human accomplishment.

Like all human beings, the Rabbis gave thought to achieving happiness in this life, but characteristically, they assumed it was a result of pursuing higher ends. They did not seek satisfaction in either deprivation or wild celebration. God's presence, the Talmud teaches, rests not on one who is idle, or gloomy, but one who experiences the joy of doing God's will (Pes. 117a). Even more definitive is the statement of a fourth-century Rabbinic sage: "There is no sadness in the presence of God" (Hag. 5b).

"Choose life" is a biblical directive; "Be happy" is not. Happiness can be an idol too, like all things that human beings worship and seek that are not Divine. "Be Holy" is the biblical directive. Holiness depends upon human beings acting in concert with God. Sacredness and not satisfaction is the end of life as traditionally conceived by Judaism. Satisfaction is important when it is not all-important. The Rabbis were not ascetics (one Rabbi goes so far as to assert that individuals will have to answer in the next world for all the pleasures they neglected to enjoy in this world! [P. T. Kidd. 4,12]), but they understood that the pursuit of happiness should contribute to, not detract from, the pursuit of holiness.

That pursuit is what we shall be tracing throughout this book. For whenever the Jewish tradition speaks of God, it speaks of how to be holy. In communication, in encounter, in imitation, in submission to and rebellion against God, holiness is found. Holiness is a greater ideal by far than happiness because it embraces struggle and sees all things—achievement, aspiration, even love—as a part of the moral drama of the world and not as life's end or sole reason for being. Holiness is greater than happiness because it is never achieved, it is ever in process, an elusive goal just beyond our reach. The ladder of holiness is built with the rungs of each human life, each worthy accomplishment, each effort at goodness. Sanctity is the only human ladder that reaches, in the biblical metaphor, to the heavens.

A relationship to God can be satisfying and at times will make one happy, but it is not that dreamed-of road to perfect contentment. Perhaps we will one day realize that such a road does not exist. If it existed, we would not need endless and disputing works on how to get there. The adjustment is required of our ideals, not our techniques. Judaism's counsel is clear: Lay the maddening chimera of constant happiness to one side and seek instead to emulate that highest prophetic ideal—to do justice, to love mercy, and to walk humbly with God.

That counsel, wise as it may be, has never been harder to heed. Concerned and thoughtful people struggle with belief, seeking a home in their own spiritual traditions, which seem strange or outmoded or simply irrelevant. Some of the obstacles are a result of historical position, obstacles of culture, language, idiom. More pervasive, however, is a gulf of vision between the modern seeker and the tradition. Some feel they can no more summon up faith in God than in any mythological creation that once captured the fancy of their youth.

Faith today is beset by problems, and there is no certain solution. Even the most resolute believer will, if his or her heart is open, admit to times of doubt and unbelief. The search for faith in one's life is a battle, alternately infuriating and enchanting, wonderful and bitterly disappointing.

But part of being fully human is asking the most important questions that confront us, asking them again and again, not letting them go until we figure out what it means to be a human being, why we were put here, whether we were put here for any reason at all.

To be sure, these questions do not always prey upon our minds. Throughout our lives, at many moments, the voice of deeper concern will be faint, perhaps unheard. When the course of life is smooth, we tend not to interrupt its gentle flow by wondering about such abrupt and awesome questions. Yet life is rarely so obliging as to permit us to forget the ultimate issues for very long. Eventually, in one form or another, questions resurface, forcing us again to confront the uneasy fact of our existence: that it will one day end, and we must formulate for ourselves some sense of why it was all worthwhile. And though these questions may not haunt our days, each of us asks them when the night comes.

2

Night and Silence

"Watchman, what of the night?"   —Isaiah 21:11

And who is the watchman? The Holy One, blessed be He.
                    —Midrash HaGadol, Exodus 12:42

Faith is grasped first by tones and mood. Before approach-
ing the Jewish conception of God, we must step back to feel
the world in which belief is born and nurtured. We need to
find words that can describe the origins of belief that lie in
silence. We have to remember by light of day how stirring
is the night.

NIGHT

We are best touched at night. The day seems harsh and real
and rational, but night—even with electric lamps and neon
splitting the dark—casts a sensitizing shade over us. There
are night thoughts and night imaginings. There are certainties of the night that can be shaken by nothing except
the coming of the dawn. Fear is a night child. So is faith.

Night is still the primal state. Solid darkness subdues
the confident bluster of our day. It is one of the infallible
reenactments of childhood, one of those times when early
years return with full clarity and force: In the darkness, we

hear something, or believe we do. External senses and internal imagination lose their separateness. The dark transcends its negations and it is no longer the absence of light. Dark is a presence, a force that returns us to an earlier time, a time of phantasms and fears. A time, perhaps stretching to now, when our estimate of the world was not so confident, when it contained things that made us shudder, and wonder. Sooner or later, the night finds us alone.

In the Jewish tradition, the world began with night. Creation, conceived in darkness, moved on to light, days, remote constellations. Night is the original state out of which the cosmos in widening circles was born. It recalls us to origins. We began as did the world, each of us in the dark, without the reassurance of a sun-spattered world. And night remains, spread throughout the Bible and the tradition, its foreboding refrain marking off rounds of time, seasons, epochs.

Prophets have often heard the word in the hushed night. How enormous the tear rent in stillness when the voice of God touches a seer in the dark! We read of that great initial vision in the covenant of Abraham: "As the sun was about to set, a deep sleep fell upon Abram, and a great dread descended upon him. And He said to Abram: 'Know well that your offspring shall be strangers in a foreign land, and they shall be enslaved and oppressed four hundred years; but I will execute judgment on their oppressors, and they shall go free . . . ' " (Gen. 15:12–14).

In the terrible dread of encroaching dark, Abraham hears the awful prophecy. The forbidding blackness has gripped the imaginations of generations. Abraham's terror will be transmuted to awe and to gratitude on that fearful night when slavery is foretold. The terrible assurance of slavery, the oppression, must be given in the night. For its obverse echo is the eighth plague, when the children of Israel are shielded by the dark at the edge of liberation.

The dread of dark surrounds and suggests Egyptian bondage, and recurs in God's appearance to Jacob. "And God came to Jacob in a vision of the night and said: 'Jacob! Jacob!' He answered, 'Here I am.' And He said, 'I am God, the God of your ancestors. Do not fear going down to Egypt, for I will make you there a great nation. I Myself will descend with you, and I Myself will bring you out from there . . .' " (Gen. 46:2–4). All the components of night are here: the fear, the destiny, the vision, the promise. Jacob will descend to Egypt, and there the night will find his descendants beleaguered, enslaved, close to despairing of the coming redemptive dawn. Jacob himself understands both the power and the foreboding of the night, for he has had dreams.

God is intimately tied to the night. The depths night touches, the conflicts it evokes in us, produce the curious combination of fear, passion, intimacy, and mystery that is the Jewish God. In the greatest dark, the dark of Egypt, redemption occurs. In the ultimate night, that of the future, redemption is promised. God moves between the poles of night, danger and promise.

Seek God at night. "I arise at midnight to praise you," writes the Psalmist (119:62). Traditions have existed for generations in Jewish pietistic circles of rising in the dead of night to sing praises to God, to augment devotion with the unreality of night, see the world bathed in enchantment and shadow; to approach the Divine when distractions of day have receded and the playthings of a coruscating world have passed briefly away.

Dark reduces to essences. Freed of vision, we see inside. Primary concerns emerge; much that seemed demanding and important is now a trick played by the light. Darkness is the black cape of the magician laid gently upon the world, until all that seemed certain vanishes, and we question comprehension itself. We can then search in a new way.

As the day is divided, along with human spirits, into light and dark, so does God divide His manifestations. We see a certain God in the day, stripped of our unreason and the suggestive anxieties of day's end. In the day, God is clearer, if equally inexplicable. Human beings perceive God differently alone, at night. Night offers inwardness, aloneness. It is when the spirit, unable to forget itself by being lost in the day or distracted, must sleep or seek. It is the time to look for the God who waits within.

"The night of watching is the Lord's" (Ex. 12:42). Now catch the receptivity of the human spirit, when God watches for signs of communication. Prayers of the night need not compete with the persistent din of daytime activity and ambition. They pierce the calm.

A dark canvas is spread across the sky. Softly, a prayer rises. Perhaps a silence makes its way to heaven.

SILENCE

Night and silence, those powerful twin evocations, suggest God because of what they create inside of us: One cannot approach God in arrogant surety; night brings the uneasiness of worry necessary for communication, the self-effacement prepared to confront that which is greater than itself. Silence is the compelling medium with which that confrontation must be expressed. Silence is necessary because there is a sublime message in the Rabbinic declaration that if all things in this world would be silent for just a moment, the ten commandments would be heard reverberating down through the ages. For the Torah, we are told, began in silence: "When God gave the Torah, no birds sang. No ox bellowed. The sea was calm. Not a creature stirred" (Ex. R. 29:9). In silence is contained the ultimate affirmation.

Without silence we are unaware of the need for true

communication, cover it with the bustle of each day's activity; so long as our scurrying is unbroken by sorrow or forced reflection, we can ignore entreaties to communicate. Silence helps one to focus, wonder, listen; it helps one to hear, since silence is never absolute. Always it contains some measure of communication. "Silence," wrote G. K. Chesterton, "is the unbearable repartee." There is nothing to answer to silence, but silence is, in itself, often the sufficient answer.

A certain kind of speaking must be done only out of silence. It is hesitant at first. One is reluctant to break the smoothness of the atmosphere. But when words finally come—measured, important or one would not permit oneself to speak them—they rush, become a torrent. Silence broken is a stream. Prayer in the middle of the night feels the burden of darkness and knows it is a brief deepened word before the dawn.

We must accustom ourselves to listen to the night. Three times in the dead of night God calls the young servant Samuel (1 Sam. 3), but Samuel does not realize it is God's call, does not know until the more practiced ear of Eli hears secondary accents of the unfolding drama. One can listen in, and to, the darkness. Currents run along the glister of stars and the stillness.

The God of the Bible speaks. But even more important, He is a God who is spoken to; who hears supplications, accusations, prayer. His action is always in question. Each prayer renews the agonizing question of Divine power unspent. But although unpredictable, He is never indifferent; although at times He seems arbitrary, He is never deaf.

He is near the intimacy of silent moments. The times of greatest communion in the prayer service are moments of silence. Words are spoken—shape is always given to Jewish devotion—but they are not spoken out loud. God inhabits these silent spaces, fills them up, makes the silence an active force, not a void. "Is there a God closer than this, that one can enter a synagogue, hide behind a pillar and whisper, and still He hears?" (Ber. 13a)

An ancient tradition has it that the verse in Psalms "Rest in the Lord" really should be translated "Be silent in the Lord" (37:7). We are only beginning to understand the ways in which these ideas—silence, night, and God—interplay in history. There are silences of the Lord, and in the Lord: the silence of God's refusing to speak, and of human beings nonetheless quietly serene in their confidence of God's deliverance. There have been periods of night in our time greater than any in history, of darkness of the human soul. Still the negative of day that night presents to the eye has sometimes highlighted glimmers of redemption, legitimate glints of hope that there may eventually be a better time. In both images—the night that has cast its murky despair over much of the age and the hints of an emerging day—we find the idea of God.

We begin with night because we cannot expect brilliance and beautiful lightness to bear faith on their wings. Belief can be burdensome as well as quickening.

That is why the exploration of faith begins with the probing of fears. Faith finds its first seeds in human incapacity and never loses the realization that its roots are sunk in dark places.

"Jacob was left alone. And a man wrestled with him until the break of dawn" (Gen. 32:25). Wrestling with another, with the night, earns Jacob the name Israel. Only by virtue of his effort and courage does he earn the right to a new name. The challenge had to take place at night, for part of this story, as commentators have argued for centuries, is Jacob's descent into his own darkness. His true struggle is internal: with the fear he feels before the encounter with his brother Esau; to overcome the self-absorption that has marred his character in the biblical account up to this point.

Jacob's battle has become a paradigm, a sublime example of wrestling with the self. He could not have emerged as Israel from an encounter with day. His brilliant talents and promise did not earn him the name. His relationship to God was not tested and tempered in the ease and assurance of his life before he fled from home. Like Abraham before him, Jacob is confronted in the night, facing the elements inside of himself that stir and surprise him, calling up reserves of strength he did not know he had.

As the sun rose on the combatants, the struggle ended. It was impossible to continue, for it was an exploration and a battle of darkness. So it has remained for each subsequent generation, and the scars of battle have remained as well; Jacob's limp reminds us that when we face ourselves we do not emerge unscathed. We are wounded by each honest confrontation with what we are and would be. Still, they are scars of inner strength and exist because we are seeking something that cannot be wrested easily from the world.

Finally, strength must be tested in the day. Jacob's bout was meaningful because he was going forth to meet his brother and his destiny. That which remains in the isolated shell of personal experience, of silence and distance, is ultimately meaningless. The philosopher Alfred N. White-head wrote that "religion is what one does with his solitude." Not for the Jew. For the Jew, religion is what one does in community, for oneself and others, in relationship and mutual aid. Solitude is the prelude, the time to practice and perfect the instrument of self for life together with others. Still, the springs of such activity are found deep inside, between the searching soul and God. That is why, like Jacob, we hope that the night will release its mystery to us, and the dawn will come.

3

Quest

But the dead know nothing; they have no recompense, for
even the memory of them has died. Their loves, their hates,
their jealousies have long since perished, and they have no
more share until the end of time. . . .

—Ecclesiastes 9:5–6

Human fears are two: the uncertainties of life and the certainty of death. The uncertainty of life is not only in disaster
and sadness; it haunts all our moments, the joyous as surely
as the tragic. At the summit of success, in the very instant
of triumph, we feel that achievement is tenuous and hope
fleeting. Behind the insecurity of living, sometimes seductive, often terrible, is finality, death. There is continuity, to
be sure: children who carry on our qualities, accomplishments that outlive us. But the unique, unrepeatable individual, the one who suffers and rejoices, who grows and
learns and changes, who reckons up the worthy and worthless in this world, is stolen by death.

"What is to be gained from my death? . . . Can dust
praise You?" asks the Psalmist (30:10), seeking to entice
God with the bribe of human worship; perhaps he will be
granted more time if it is used to glorify God in prayer. But
the decree is inevitable, and the only battle is a skirmish
over the border inches of a few years, a bit more comfort.
Perhaps certain individuals sedately accept death, but as a
society, a species, we wage a titanic struggle against its

appetite. How much human activity is designed to delay death! A hospital is the spangled, solid monument to the overt struggle, taking hostilities to the front. But there is also exercise, diet, the vast ingenuity devoted to accident prevention of all sorts, coiffures and cosmetics: our unceasing struggle to look young is but another frantic and even angry way of insisting how far we are from the end. Acutely conscious of death, cognizant of its inescapability, we fight at every turn, seek, heroically or pitifully, to reverse that which cannot be changed.

The effort is as enormous as it is hopeless. "Making something of your life" is a way of staving off death, of insisting that it will not rob us of that great gift, the sign of having lived. Something will stand—a testimonial, an organization, a name in a book, a child, some memories. It is not death alone, horrible as it sometimes seems, but the inevitability of oblivion, the not-having-been that gnaws or rages inside us. Each individual, in different accents and inflections, in all languages and forms, speaks the same two small words to the universe: Notice. Stay.

This is the pain of love and the check on joy. At moments of intense love there is also an ache somewhere in the center of the soul. Because the beloved will, like the lover, not always stay. Because attachment carries with it the whispered prefiguration of loss. Because before even love itself, the first fact is its impermanence.

Spending time with someone who is loved and dying is a reminder that nothing can be made to stay. For it is not only the person who will be gone. However tightly we hold his or her hand, however deeply we breathe of his or her presence and essence, memories gently fade, presence ebbs away in the course of time. Even knowing this, we cannot impress others deeply enough on ourselves to make them stay as they are in life. Human memory is too fragile a vessel to carry the vitality of a person. The immediacy of presence is as nothing else. Next to being, memory is a delicate thread, hazily seen, indifferently spun, slack and worn.

I remember someone I love. The first meaning of that sentence is that the loved one is gone.

A painful paradox of our age is that all the advances we have made in retention and retrieval of information have not advanced human identity over oblivion. People do not feel more confident of remembrance than they did one hundred or one thousand years ago. We can preserve on tape, on film, on microchip; we call upon scores of names and details and lineage; we have catapulted past the imperfections of human memory. And still we fear forgetting, and being forgotten.

For being recorded and recollected is not the same as being remembered. Recording preserves the outline, not the essence. Vital statistics fit snugly in footnotes and on tombstones, but they tell us nothing of a life. Names and birth dates and social security numbers, the vast aggregation of personal fact does not touch me or capture what I am. Why do we feel more anonymous while information about us accumulates every day? Why can we not understand that we are in some ways more indestructibly preserved than at any time in human history? Because the human being is lost, and only the dust of detail remains.

Science and research nudge at the edge of the biological life span, granting greater health, some more time. Technology busies itself ensuring that the names of those who are gone will be retained on files and forms, as part of opinion polls and statistically sound historical generalizations. Predictably, no one is reassured. For only so long as there remains someone who knew *me*, the individual, the untransmittable essence of another person, am I remembered. All the preservational apparatus in the world will not tell me what someone whom I never knew was truly like. People are more than two- or even three-dimensional. The fourth dimension is how they are in life, in quickened, breathing, unreproducible life.

This is not a new dilemma. The academic lexicon swells with terms like "angst," "dread," "nothingness." All the terms have been used before, all the fears expressed. The danger of an intellectual fashion is that shrillness and obscure terminology will forfeit its point. In the middle of this century despair was in vogue, and existential suffering chic. But at bottom the concern was not fashionable, it was fundamental. No matter how it is phrased, whether in abstruse jargon or everyday language, the fear of death has been with us as long as has death itself, and the desire for meaning as long as human beings have lived. Midrash Haneelam puts it simply: "When one remembers that he is dust and will return to dust, everything seems hollow and vain." The terminology varies. The problem is the one great constant of the human condition.

Death and loss cannot be changed or transcended. It is useless to speak of a "cure" for fears of oblivion. We make gestures of preservation, believing that we have truly lived before and so will again, or even imagining that the fountain of youth is now located in some laboratory. Human credulity has always expanded when puffed up with promises of immortality, although the certainty of failure has shadowed the search. Still we continue to explore, for the impulse to cure is too great, and the defeat too final to accept. Some of our attempts are pitiful, others worthy. None is a final answer.

OUTRUNNING DEATH

There are two basic strategies for outrunning death. One is to seek the perpetuation of the individual. This is one spark of the enormous investment in children, the continuation of the name. Why are parents so delighted when told their children resemble them? The "perpetuation project" is here seen plain: if your child is like you, then at death you do not die. In an earlier age, you could leave a hereditary plot of land, something that was certain to be tied to the family name and heritage. A piece of earth, the importance of which is evident in ancient and medieval tales, was a palpable presence that would carry on the name and legacy of its owner. The connection of family and land was primal, essential, an assurance of continuity. Now the mobility of a modern age forces reliance on less solid transfers: name, character, resemblance, possessions.

Many hope their mark will be left in another field as well, in business, academics, politics, or art. The impulse to create an empire that will last forever is not so different from the impulse to create a business with one's name loudly lettered on the top of the building. It is the creation of an individual memorial to subvert the censorship of death. The pyramids of Egypt are not only megalomaniacal monuments; they are in some sense what all of us would like, given the resources: a giant tombstone that will contradict our very death by making its marker last for the ages. Ultimately it cannot work, of course, as we are so eloquently told in Shelley's poem "Ozymandias," where a traveler comes upon a pedestal that reads: "My name is Ozymandias, king of kings: / Look on my works, ye Mighty, and despair!" The traveler notices that "Nothing beside remains. Round the decay / Of that colossal wreck, boundless and bare / The lone and level sands stretch far away." Time has stolen the grandeur of Ozymandias too.

Whether through the love and care lavished on children or by other less intimate, wonderful accomplishments, so long as influence lives the individual survives. To outdistance death one need only to continue to have some impact on the world left behind. One still dies, of course, but oblivion has been cheated if influence remains. We have not been wiped out. We existed, and in some small corner of the world evidence remains of this supremely important fact. It is not enough, to be sure, but it is something. When in the Talmud a Rabbi quotes his dead teacher, it is said that the teacher's "lips are murmuring in the grave." To speak on after death is an immortality of sorts, but it can never be enough, as we hear in the following:

> When the great sage Rav died, his students went to pay their last respects. Upon returning from the funeral they stopped to eat by the river Danak. When the time arrived for grace after the meal, they could not decide upon the proper form of grace. Rav Ada stood up and made a second tear of mourning in his garment and cried out, "Rav is gone and we have not even learned from him all the laws of blessing after meals!" (Ber. 42b, 43a)

For all that Rav had contributed, at each moment there was reason to mourn anew, for he was gone. The first tear in Rav Ada's garment was for the loss that he felt upon hearing of Rav's death. The second tear was for all the times in the future when he would need Rav's wisdom and guidance, and it would not be there.

The other solution to the fear of oblivion is precisely the reverse of individual perpetuation: extinguishing the individual conscience, which is anyway doomed. We know the first solution, maintaining some piece of oneself, cannot ultimately work because the influence and memory of any person will eventually fade. The alternative is to be swept up in some great whole, whether a societal mass movement or the presumed Oneness of the universe. If everyone marches together, none need march alone.

This is an approach with great attraction, and it seems to show a becoming humility. One does not arrogantly seek personal perpetuation, but rather remembrance in the service of one or another cause. In terms often applied to a mystical experience, one becomes a drop in the vast ocean. The ocean, of course, will remain, even when the solitary drop has long since been dried away by the sun.

Yet this solution is tarnished by the terrors of the past century. The consequences of submerging personality into a gigantic collective can be terrifying. We have discovered, particularly in this bloody age, that when people abdicate their individual wills, the result can be disaster. To see giant crowds marching in lockstep with the same blank expressions, prepared to die and to kill in the service of some greater "Ideal," makes us shudder with the awful recognition of the genocidal face of nazism or Stalinism. It appears that atop the "greater Oneness" there is often the "greater one" who is, if not bloodthirsty, frequently exploitative of the minions prepared to crush their consciences on the wheel of the collective.

Destroying the variety and integrity of the individual is a crime. Part of the glory of creation is, as the Rabbis put it, that while a human king mints faces on coins and each looks the same, the King of Kings, God, creates people and each one is different (Mishna San. 4:5). In one of the most poignant and direct declarations in all of literature, God begins His message to the prophet Ezekiel by declaring: "Son of man, stand upon your feet that I may speak to you" (2:1). Ezekiel must rise, swell to the height of his human dignity. When human beings are prepared to stand upon their own two feet, to present themselves in the plentitude of their abilities and integrity, God will speak. Stand upon your own two feet, you who will die, and cope somehow with your fate.

This insistence upon individuality is characteristic of the

Jewish tradition. Not only is it affirmed by the parade of exceptional individuals—biblical, Talmudic, medieval, and modern—whose very uniqueness is celebrated, but it is affirmed by the mythic recounting of creation in terms of a single individual. The Bible depicts God as having created each individual human being in His image. Each person is a different embodiment of the Divine spark. In the Jewish view, to deny that individuality, to submerge it in another, or others, is to go against the very intent of creation. Judaism rejected the renunciation practiced by other cultures, the deliberate cultivation of passivity, because the assertion of one's uniqueness is essential. Among the many different attempts to deal with the death of the individual, avoiding becoming an individual was an option spurned by Jews and Judaism.

Of course, individuality is not the same as egocentrism. Not arrogance but fidelity to one's being is the watchword. Some seek to perpetuate themselves by caring only for themselves, enveloping the self with a tender, ever vigilant regard that ignores others. For this the Rabbis have some very harsh words. Not only is humility reckoned by the Rabbis as "the greatest of all virtues," but God Himself declares that He cannot coexist with the arrogant (Sotah 5a). In fact, one Midrash says that the Messiah will not come until arrogance is no more (San. 98a). The modern obsession with self, while it may be in part a reaction to the fear of death, is certainly no solution. To love oneself, contrary to the secret suspicion many of us nurture, is not to ensure that one will exist forever.

Yet no matter how exquisite the balance between self-regard and humility, between earthly achievement and exalted values, the question of death remains. Despite the proliferation of strategies, there is no answer. There cannot be an "answer" to death, which is why there are so many answers, so many gurus, secular and religious, willing to offer themselves and their cause as the anodyne for fear. But we must still, each of us, die alone. And the stark force of that fate cannot be washed away.

Even if there is no answer, the resolute bleakness of the problem might be assuaged. Rather than search for solutions, we should cast about to lighten the human burden. The terrific freight of being mortal cannot be unloaded, but perhaps carrying it can be rendered a bit easier. There is a way in which faith has sought for centuries, however tentatively, to ease death's sting. We no longer live in a world in which belief is the sole bearer of human aspiration, and would not wish to return there. We cannot go back in any case—history does not shed its skin. Nonetheless, an exploration of faith can help deepen whatever projects enrich our lives. Like all confrontations in the face of death, faith may seem at times hollow and difficult to sustain. Still, the depth of faith, should we achieve it, is often proportional to the pain undergone in the course of searching. Today *bitachon,* the traditional Hebrew term for trust in God, makes its stand not on unimpaired certainty, but on the softer ground of trial and hope.

THE POSSIBILITIES OF BELIEF

Faith seeks to strip the ultimacy of death. Given a perfect remembrance, a place where all who have lived remain unforgotten, a master memory in the universe, death is not the final editor of human aspiration. Over and against the fear of death there is the possibility of ultimate preservation and renewal. In other words, there is God.

God is the *beginning* of a partial answer that human beings have to death. *Zochair Kol Hanishkachot:* God remembers all the forgotten. There is no forgetting before God. Every person, achievement, deed, is touched by eternity.

There is no lost or wasted word in the unredeemed epic of human history.

Historians once wrote books that focused almost exclusively upon the actions of rulers and nobility, thinking that deeds of exceptional individuals reflect the collective fate of humanity. So one could read of kings and courtiers, but the life of the average person was at best a blur of occupational categories or plague statistics. Of late, more attention has been paid to the documentable concerns and livelihood of the masses of unnamed people, the grand gray commoners of history. Average people escaped our notice for so long that we must wonder about the mechanisms and caprices of preservation. All those years passed and the memories of most of humanity were not even investigated by those trained to do so. What will be our fate?

We are dependent upon the whims of history for what we can recall; sometimes the most improbable items are preserved. We know the Etruscans by their tombs, the Sumerians by their laundry lists. We can work only with what has survived. Who is to tell what will remain tomorrow, in the next century, of the lives we live? It has been aptly remarked of the computer that it has not only an impeccable memory, but flawless forgetfulness. One push of a button and all can be erased. Much of what seems imperishable to us today may be unknown tomorrow. Who knows what will remain? The tides of time do not signal which sandscrapers they will wash away.

In God each individual is recalled in his or her uniqueness. This is the assurance we grope for in those fortunate moments when we succeed in finding in ourselves a center of faith. Personal history, individuality, live on in their multicolored hues. No action is so trivial as to escape record. This is the religious response to the moving words of the poet Gray's famed "Elegy Written in a Country Church-yard," where he meditates on the anonymity that is the lot of most of humanity:

> *Let not Ambition mock their useful toil,*
> *Their homely joys, and destiny obscure;*
> *Nor Grandeur hear with a disdainful smile*
> *The short and simple annals of the poor . . .*
>
> *Full many a gem of purest ray serene,*
> *The dark unfathom'd caves of ocean bear:*
> *Full many a flower is born to blush unseen,*
> *And waste its sweetness on the desert air.*

The blush is not unseen, the sweetness not wasted. What Wordsworth, in the generation following Gray, called "That best portion of a good man's life,— / His little, nameless, unremembered, acts / Of kindness and of love" are remembered. They are recorded. There is no forgetting before God.

The metaphor for God's memory changes. For centuries, as depicted in the liturgy of Yom Kippur, the Day of Atonement, it was the *"Sefer Chaim,"* the book of life. In that capacious book, all one's deeds, private and public, were written down. Today, in a far different era, we are likely to think of it (as it has commonly been represented in plays and books) as a film that plays back all the events of our lives. The particular representation is unimportant. The idea is everything: All we do, all we are, is vitally preserved, not frozen in memory as in amber, a still pose that mocks the motion and heat of life. We exist in memory as in time, filled to overflowing with the individuality of our essence, with being.

This does not "cure" death. The promise of remembrance

cannot wipe out the infamous sting. Agonies of oblivion remain for all, the great as well as the "common man." One of the most beautiful passages in Jewish literature is the Midrashist's description of the death of the greatest prophet of the Jewish tradition, Moses. Not only on account of the fear of being forgotten did Moses struggle, but because life was filled with promise he had not yet realized—to walk in the land to which he had brought the people. The logical, seemingly inevitable culmination of Moses' life was stolen away. In the dark pathos and bittersweet resolution of Moses' death scene as told by the Rabbis, all the themes of death, memory, and God are interwoven in a remarkable way.

When Moses realized that his death had been decreed, he fasted, put on sackcloth, and drew a small circle on the ground. Then he stood inside of the circle and proclaimed before God: "I will not stir from this spot until You reverse Your decree." Moses continued to lament and pray before God, until the heavens and earth—the entire order of nature—trembled.

God decreed that Moses' prayer go unanswered; his fate had been decided. But so powerful did Moses' prayers become, like a sword which rends everything it touches, that all the gates of heaven had to be sealed to prevent the supplication from penetrating to the throne of the Almighty.

Still, Moses prayed, pleading with God: "Master of the universe, You know how hard I strived to teach the people of Your words and will. I journeyed with them, contended with them, and now that they are to enter the land will You exclude me from their joy? Is this the recompense for all my struggle?" God answered only, "The time of your death has come."

Moses would not cease praying, reminding God of their time together: "Master of the universe, remember that day when You revealed Yourself to me, speaking to me from the burning bush. Recall the forty days and nights we were together on Mount Sinai, where I learned Your law to teach to the people. I beg of You—do not now hand me over to the angel of death." God calmed Moses' fears with a heavenly voice that said, "Do not be afraid. The time comes to all mortals to die. I Myself will attend to your burial."

Upon hearing those words, Moses stood up and sanctified himself like the angels. God Himself came down from the very heights of heaven to take away the soul of Moses. And God took away the soul of His servant Moses with a kiss. And God wept.

(Combined from Deut. R. 11, Midrash Petirat Moshe, and parallels)

In various versions of the Midrash this scene is much expanded. The components remain essentially the same. Moses cannot be fully reconciled to death. He mourns and pleads. In one version of the story, Moses physically fights off an angel sent by God to reclaim his soul! God finally bolts the heavens because Moses summons all his power to struggle against the inevitable lot of being human. For Moses, as the Rabbis knew, death was no sweeter or easier than it is for the more pedestrian run of humanity. The greatest prophet, like the humblest pauper, is not exempt from fear. The man of God too trembles at the prospect of being no more.

Moses is given the comfort of being taken by God. His death is not so much a finality as a separation. Still, it is painful enough. Even after such a life, the prospect of death is sufficiently agonizing to cause this servant of the Lord, whom the Bible depicts as a tower of faith and strength, to offer anguished cries of injustice, to plead, to cry. But the strange softness at the end of the Midrash is suggestive of something deeper. It eases, this Divine kiss, the unyielding edges of death. Moses dies too soon. That is his tragedy and it cannot be changed. He dies in the arms of eternity, and that is his comfort and his hope.

To die too soon is a tragedy known to more than patri- archs and prophets. As the Midrash teaches, "No one leaves this world with even half of his desires fulfilled" (Eccl. R. 1:13). The proper biblical span, based upon the life of Moses, was set at 120 years. This symbolic number says, with the fullness of realism, that we all die too soon. Even when the end is accepted with apparent equanimity, it is, after all, the equanimity of inevitability. There is no choice. Death has prepared the path for acceptance by taking others whom one loves. It gradually strips capacity and appetite, smoothing the way with the persistence of pain and physical decline.

DENIALS AND AFFIRMATIONS

Since it is the body that obviously, visibly decays and dies, some traditions have been led to fear or denigrate the phys- ical being. Yet this is not the way of Judaism. For to do this is to refuse a gift on the grounds that the gift will one day disappear. Better, saner is to understand that transience governs all.

Lo Amut Ki Echyeh, wrote the Psalmist: "I will not die, but live" (118:17). Commenting on the seeming redun- dancy of that verse, the Chasidic leader the Maggid of Mezeritch said it teaches "I shall not die while I am alive." There is time enough to die. The answer to death is not to invite its reign while there is still life.

The path of extinguishing desires, of resignation, enables one to feel death not as an end, but as the final, slight step in a process consciously pursued one's entire life. Gradually the élan vital, the vital force of living, is quieted and quenched, so that when death looms, it is greeted as a fellow spirit. To the Jewish way of thinking, the shame of a life ill-lived is not only in having wasted time wanting that which one could not have, but in *not having pursued that which one could have had, should have had.* The Chasidic teacher Rabbi Bunam once commented that those who are intellectual often lose faith, those who are sociable are often overfond of physical pleasures, and those who are pious tend toward egotism. Perplexed, one of his disciples asked, "If each of these is bad, for what should one strive?" The Rabbi answered: "To be all of these combined."

Every aspect of life can be sacred, and each instant, no matter the activity, *can* be holy. Upon the death of his master, Menachem Mendle of Kotzk was asked what had been most important to the teacher whom he had just lost. He thought briefly and replied, "Whatever he was doing at the moment."

What can be done by one who is committed to the fullness of life? To have had a full life does not always reconcile one to death. At times the fuller one's experience, the more bitter its end, as we saw above with Moses. In the icy inevitability of death, resented no matter the nature of one's life, is the most immediate argument for the need of a personal God. There is some comfort to be had in the certainty of memory, the fullness of God's understanding. Such beliefs are, in the medical terminology that suggests itself when discussing death, not curative, but palliative.

Palliative measures do more than just relieve pain. They free the patient for other things. In the conviction of meaning, human potential is decisively liberated. If death, however painful, is not the derisive mocker of all ambition and accomplishment, then human beings can strive toward a goal with the assurance that the pursuit is not all wasted. Meaninglessness, not pain, robs human effort of its sheen of fulfillment. If we are a teeming mass of finite creatures, observed only by each other, doomed to a common oblivion, where is the glory in reaching beyond the pitiful emptiness of our passing estate? Although we can depict the struggle as somehow noble, it is also fixed—death will always win in the end. It is this abiding certainty that forces us to question all the meanings we create along the way. As the Midrash notes, we are all born with our fists clenched, as if to say "There is so much to hold on to in this world," but we leave with our hands open, as if to say "I can take nothing with me" (Eccl. R. 5:14). When it is time to go, hard-won possessions, both moral and material, must be relinquished, and are ours no more.

If we are given the chance of affirmation, however, life is enriched and death not quite so hollow. The possibility of deeper meaning does exist beneath the veneer of pointlessness. The affirmation works on many levels: physical, psychological, intellectual. Cause and worth are newly supported by confidence in God, and themselves lead to God in other ways.

THE PULL OF
JUSTICE AND CONCERN

Death is the most obvious and insistent, but not the only pull toward a reliance on God. The burden of living in this world, knowing its pain, is too great for feeling people to bear alone. There is too much, always, battering our sensibilities, crying out for empathy, restoration, and hope. At times the world seems designed not to arouse compassion, but to foster insensitivity as the only recourse enabling one to go on. Is there a soul so sturdy that it can look on all this carnage and stay whole? In a world such as this, who can deny the wisdom of the Kotzke Rebbe's beautiful epigram "The only whole heart is a broken one"? There is no feeling heart in this world that is not broken. Still, to survive we must be callous. Or certain that we do not have to bear it all alone.

The ballast that keeps human beings weighted to this world is common effort. The feeling that there is shared anguish, and shared efforts at alleviation, is vital. Each human being must participate. That is the wisdom in the Jewish law mandating that the first thing a beggar must do, upon receiving charity, is donate a portion to another more needy than he. But human effort, however sporadically noble and ennobling, is not enough. We are too small. Our fears too great.

That is why there is need of a Divine "ally." People are an uneasy amalgam of competence and insufficiency, gentleness and savagery. The smooth assurance that our better side will triumph is a faith that has been belied repeatedly by human history. The preceding century saw the dawning of a confident faith that human beings would improve, march from moral sunrise to brightest day. It appeared that the progress we made in intellectual endeavors, in technology and social sciences, was an anticipation of a great, generalized advance. We know, sadly, through the wrenching history of the last seventy years, that this faith was disastrously naive. Human beings left to their own devices will not steadily improve, stride toward a moral perfection. Rather, the phenomenal improvement in technology merely permits us to accelerate the carnage spurred by bestial impulses that have not dulled, it seems, since the dawn of time.

Here as elsewhere, the allegory of the Tower of Babel is instructive. The technology of the workmen led to hubris, to the assurance that they could build up to heaven itself.

The Rabbis imagine them so intent upon completing the building that if a human being fell and was killed, no one noticed. But if a brick fell and was broken, they sat and wept (Pirke de-R.El. 24). The parallels to our own time, and our own equations of the value of human life versus that of technological progress, are terribly apt. Skill alone does not make us kinder.

With a consciousness of the Divine, the chance to mitigate our savagery is better. Balzac may have been making a cynical aside when, in *Père Goriot,* he wrote: "Perhaps only believers in God do good in secret." Yet it is true that God's providential concern is both comforting and salutary for moral sensibility. It helps to know one does not act in a vacuum. But it does *not* help if God is the distant, disapproving Judge of so many misconceived believers and misled students of religion. It is not a "religious" conception to see God as the malicious Deity whose Divine intelligence is continually occupied with devising new and more horrible punishments to inflict on His errant creations.*

All that we have said above makes sense only if we assume a certain kind of God. A stern and unforgiving Deity or an indifferent God would not be a comfort, could not begin to address the fears we share. Far too many are convinced that this is the God of the Jewish tradition. But in Judaism, the true quest is for a God who is close.

THE PERSONAL
GOD OF TRADITION

The classical Jewish search for God is a search for a personal God. The majestic remoteness of the philosophic God has not been *totally* alien to the search: "For My ways are not as

---

* For more on this subject, see chapter 8.

your ways nor My thoughts as your thoughts" (Is. 55:8). God is clearly not the same as human beings: "To whom, then, can you liken God? What form compare to Him?" (Is. 40:18) But the biblical God of Sinai spoke to each individual alike. The Rabbis teach that God's commands were presented to each person in accord with his or her ability to comprehend. "Rabbi Levi said: God appeared to Israel in infinite images reflecting the appearance of each individual, and all felt personally addressed" (Pes. de-R.K. 12:25). In the moment of greatest revelation, at the spiritual zenith of Israelite history, the God who manifested Himself at Sinai was a personal God. A God who spoke to individuals as well as to the collective.

Ultimacy is no bar to intimacy. God is also the Creator, the ineffable, unreachable, supreme spirit. But even those characteristics that seem most exalted in God are bound to the deep personhood of the Creator of all things.

To ask for a just God is to care for justice not only for the world, but for oneself and one's family and one's neighbor. Any general description of God's qualities is also a statement about our lives and the way we wish them to be. To say that God is limitless may seem an abstract intellectual statement about the qualities of an omnipotent Deity. But it is rooted in the personal, in the perception of God in the world, in the life of the believer: God who created the cosmos, in all its distant and magnificent array, created the earth upon which we walk and till and grow, and the sun that, from whatever distant berth, lights and warms our way.

Despite the inclinations of philosophy, with its love of the abstract, it is no advance in intellectual sophistication to suppose a God of ultimate transcendence, who cannot be thought of or addressed in terms of closeness. A God who encompasses all things must have poetry, too. To depersonalize God is no service to God or to human beings. Indeed, it is precisely because God is everywhere, seemingly an abstract philosophical attribute, that a believer in Him is never a stranger, no matter where he or she may be (P.T. Ber. 9:1).

"The fool says in his heart there is no God" (Ps. 14:1). The heart, not the head, is the seat of denial. For it is also the seat of affirmation. From the outside, to be sure, faith can look irrational, even ludicrous. The Chasidic parable has it right: When you see someone swaying in prayer it appears foolish. But you must imagine that you are passing a glass house where music is playing and those inside are dancing. You can see them swaying, but you cannot hear the music, and so the motion appears irrational. One who sways in prayer hears a special harmony. If others cannot hear it, that does not mean there is no music.

The quest for a personal God does not begin in reasoned affirmation about the prime mover, the first cause, or any of the rationalistic attempts to demonstrate Divine existence. The quest for a personal God begins in the heart. It must embrace the intellect, of course. Judaism in particular is a highly intellectual tradition, where reason and rigorous thought have a central place. Still, the structure of argument is raised upon a foundation of conviction, and one can no more understand that conviction by reason alone than one can understand a great painting by analyzing pigments. There must be more: sensitivity, sensibility, poetry.

Searching for a personal God involves both a lack and an abundance. We feel a lack of wholeness. This feeling may lead us to a certainty that there is no greater whole, that fragmentation and happenstance rule. Or it may persuade us that there must be more than this, more than we see—that there is an above and a beyond. Is there, in the very limitations of our intellects, an apprehension of something more powerful, closer to infinity and eternity? A human being, mired in the now, raising his or her feet from the sands of the present only by straining the intellectual musculature, can perhaps sense that every limitation in this world suggests its own transcendence, that in our very sluggishness there is the suggestion of a more comprehensive mind, a more embracing power. In certain receptive (or perhaps misguided) moments, there is an undefeatable sense that this cannot be all. This cosmos is too large and we, for all of our glory, are too small. There may be other life, but it will not answer the question, it will only enlarge it. Can we and this other species, these other thousand species, be all? Is there no ultimacy above this varied pageant?

There is realization in the search, a peculiar gift of seeing. Like any important perspective, it must be wrested from the world, fought for to be felt. Millions of people had seen rocks fall before Galileo saw them fall with a different end in view. Millions of people had seen the sun rise before Abraham saw it borne aloft on the finger of God. With belief, with the concerted attempt to open the self to God, there is a chance of hearing in the world tones of personal address.

Apprehension of an intimate God comes in part from a world in which one feels individually addressed. The world "speaks" to each of us. It speaks not in the undifferentiated notes of an impersonal natural beauty, but in the direct address of nature.

There is nothing mystical or improbable in this feeling. It is the extension of kinship, the conception of unity. The world, if one creation, is inextricably bound together. Creation is a coherent work of art.

The Rabbis tell many stories of the significance of all creation. All creatures have their place and purpose. Even at the crowning hour of human history, we are reminded that we are but a part of a vast panorama of creation. In pondering why God created man last in the biblical account, the Midrash offers two answers: "Why was man created last? So that all would be ready for him. God acted as a host who first prepared the banquet and then had His guest arrive. On the other hand, the timing of creation is a reminder in arrogant moments that we are of humble origins, for the gnat preceded us in the order of creation" (San. 38a).

We are all part of one immense canvas whose connections are so intricate that we are but beginning to understand them. The religious view is to rise above the art enough to see how much one is a part of it, and to see in it—and so in oneself—the hand of the Artist.

Some have tried to fashion this as an intellectual proof of God, but it is not. It is grounded not in reasoning, but in artistic sensibility, in the appreciation of beauty and the desire for its completion. Commenting on a verse in the beginning of the book of Samuel from Hannah's prayer of thanksgiving for her newborn child, the Rabbis subtly alter Hannah's Hebrew words "There is no rock like our God" so that they read "There is no artist like our God" (Ber. 10a). The Rabbis frequently play language games to make a point, demonstrating their own artistry at the same time as they depict God as the ultimate Artist. In all the models for viewing God, perhaps this is the most true to our everyday experience: God is perceived in the brush strokes of creation: the froth rhythmically bubbling up on a white beach, the wrinkled, changing faces of a range of mountains, or, as in Hannah's prayer, the creation of human life.

One impulse in the search for a personal God is indeed the God of nature and creation. But even artistic appreciation is abstract compared with the yearning from which the original impulse toward God grows. The Jewish tradition reminds human beings that they are both beast and angel.

"Choose life": those are the immemorial words of Deuteronomy. It is not only in goodness, but in the infinite space that separates good from evil, the space of choice, that God can be found. Discovery and exploration of God in the Jewish tradition will always return to the most important arena, which is not the world of natural beauty, but the conduct of human beings.

Nowhere is God so needed by human beings and so vividly depicted by the tradition as in the decisions of human life: personal, interpersonal, societal, global. Dealing with other people is the first and most important measure of respect for or disregard of God.

Without the ambivalence and the insistent burden of choice, the voice of God is muted. *Mitzvah,* "command,"* is not a coercive fiat. Divine command is an insistence that human beings recognize the proper choice, but choice it remains. Choosing wrong, deciding upon evil and savagery, is a human prerogative and an everlasting theme of history. Choice is the gift; using it aright is the gratitude.

Guidance, comfort, and governance—the search for all three has its place in the quest to find, in Jewish tradition, a "personal" God. Naturally there are other manifestations of God in Jewish tradition: God the Divine monarch, God the lawgiver, God who concerns Himself with the survival and ultimate redemption of humanity.

Yet no interpretation of God is compelling that does not begin with the recognition that God is first and foremost the designer of human beings, the Creator whose concern and knowledge are bound up inextricably with the work of His hands. "Lord, you have examined me and know me . . . I am awesomely, wonderfully made" (Ps. 139:1, 14). In our

---

* Although commonly translated as "good deed" (a secondary, colloquial meaning), *mitzvah* in fact comes from the root meaning "command," and the *mitzvot* are considered commandments in the Jewish tradition.

very selves, our existence, the intricate and nearly unfathomable creation of the human spirit, is the first glimmering of acknowledgment of God.

We have advanced several "ports of entry" to God in this chapter, all of them aspects of the quest: God is sought by some in moral considerations, aesthetic estimations, in creation, in choice, law, and tradition. There are other ways as well. We have seen that behind many, perhaps most, of these approaches is the painful and unavoidable reality of death, a reality that haunts and mocks human life. Yet, although we have argued here for human finitude as an argument to lead us to God, it can also lead away from God, as pain, death, and tragedy make the reality of God more and more remote. Some of these issues will be addressed in more detail later in this book.

We proceed, however, with the possibility that thought and discussion will yield some help and hope. Different answers will appeal to different people at various times in their lives. A religious tradition seeks to keep the channels open.

Between human beings and God, understanding is reciprocal; God wishes to be sought as well as to seek. Pointedly did Abraham Joshua Heschel title two of his theological meditations *Man's Quest for God* and *God in Search of Man*. Neither is sufficient alone. Like lovers, human beings and God constantly meditate on each other and seek each other's presence.

In the famous formulation of Martin Buber, God "cannot be expressed, only addressed." No description of God or of one's relationship with Him can take the place of an honest attempt to encounter God on one's own. It is only against this background that we can feel the urgency of redemptive hope.

The Jewish tradition is an instrument of and guide for the search. Embodying an ancient expression of the human quest for God, it brings together rites, ideas, and history in service of this same goal, to join humanity and God. The Rabbis saw the Torah as the bridge tossed across the chasm that separates the earth from heaven. For us today there are many paths forged by the Jewish tradition that allow each, given determination and good fortune, to join those two distinct domains. We need to begin by asking the tradition, For what do we search? What is God in the Jewish tradition and how does He touch human lives? And where do we look to encounter the Jewish God?

4

The God of the Midrash

Aggadah [Midrashic legend] captures the heart.
—Shabbat 87a

Where in the Jewish tradition does the search for a personal
God begin? Where is the treasury of images, imaginings,
and piety that will act as a spur to each individual search?
How unrestrained can one's conception be while remaining
within the confines of the Jewish tradition? To attempt
answers to these questions, we must look at the Rabbinic
God—God as envisioned in the Talmud and Midrash. For
although the Jewish tradition is founded upon the Bible, it
is the Bible as interpreted by the Rabbis.

"The Rabbis" denotes the Rabbis of the Talmudic period, roughly 100 B.C.E. to 600 C.E. The major Rabbinic
centers were in Babylonia and Israel. The many writings
bequeathed to us by these shapers of the Jewish tradition fall
into two basic categories: law (*Halacha*) and interpretation
and legend (*Aggadah*—Midrashic tales). In this chapter, and
in this book, we are dealing primarily with Midrash, which
begins as a rule with the biblical text, interpreting a verse
or a word, but then ranges far, over the entirety of human
concern, weaving elaborate legends and offering terse epigrams, all the while refining and molding Jewish faith.

Midrash is the free verse of theology. Its rules are flexible, and its aim is less shape and system than beauty and meaning. There is a certain loose rigor to the style; Midrash is hardly formless. But in its leaps of symbol and rich reference, it is suggestive, not systematic—the literature of a people who feel God along the heart before trying to rationalize and conceptualize Him.

To elicit the attitude of the Midrash on any given issue can be a daunting task. There is little general exposition. Stories and epigrams take the place of theological analysis. Still, in the accumulation of assertions and piquant detail a general picture emerges, vital and invigorating, of the Rabbis' sense of their tradition and their God.

One cannot speak with full confidence of a "Rabbinic God" unless the discussion is hedged about with caveats and chronology. The Talmudic Rabbis spanned many hundreds of years and thousands of individuals, temperaments, insights, and arguments. Yet certain themes do unmistakably emerge from their writings and ruminations. We are not concerned here with a scholarly taxonomy of Rabbinic theology. That task has been undertaken repeatedly by eminent scholars, and the work continues. We want the emotive essence of the Rabbinic God. We want to know its importance for our own lives, to look for the God of the Rabbis in their prayer and poetry. We seek their personal God, so that He may perhaps, translated into a different tongue and time, become our own.

The initial certainty is that however difficult the search, the One sought is near. God is present to the worshiper, so close that prayers are always heard, as close, in the Talmudic image, as the mouth is to the ear (Ber. 13a).

God's closeness affords the opening for all the Rabbinic description that follows. It will be clear that the daring imagery of the Rabbis would be impossible with a distant Deity. For all of God's remote majesty, He is still *in* the world, and it is this that offers the opportunity for intimacy. In the philosophical parlance that was so foreign to the Rabbis themselves, God is not only transcendent, but immanent. Or, as the Midrash has it, "While God's face is above, his heart is down below" (Song of Songs Rabbah 4, 4:9).

That God has no form and is not seen is no bar to intimacy. For such a God is everywhere, never far from the reach of a prayer or petition. In the Jewish tradition, which so cherishes words, God must be ever present to hear. "A listening ear" is one Rabbinic designation for God; He will hear the cries of human beings. As we learn more about the vastness of the cosmos, the cavernous space in which our tiny globe seems swallowed up, it is hard to imagine that we are heard. The immensity of what exists dwarfs us and mocks, to the modern mind, our swaggering pretension that what we say can matter. To the Rabbis the certainty of being heard is fundamental. In contrast to T. S. Eliot's despairing image "human voices wake us, and we drown," in the Jewish tradition, it is human voices that save us, that throw us the rope to tug us back to the shore. Let one but pray in a whisper, and he or she is heard.

The marvel of words can serve as a barrier as well as a boon. Words both make understanding possible and obscure the message. A wit once claimed that human beings were given speech to conceal their thoughts. Cognizant of the misleading nature of speech, the Rabbis had a sense of God that was deeper than words. God was the foundation of their life and soul, and early on, the Jewish tradition recognized the impossibility of speaking adequately about Him. As the beautiful imagery of the Akdamuth, a poetic prayer, puts it, "Were the skies made of parchment, all the reeds quills, all the seas and waters made of ink, and every inhabitant of earth a scribe," the glories of God still could not be adequately described. Equally impossible, however, is to maintain silence.

The burden of the Rabbinic message is often and rightly described in terms of ethical monotheism—one God and the moral implications of that idea. But the Rabbis were also bringing a message of *personal monotheism*. One God and what that means for the individual human being. One God and the unutterable majesty of His essence. One God who cares for His creations, and how that caring speaks to human fear and longing.

For all the limitations of speech, in the battle for recognition of God's sovereignty, words were the weapons the Rabbis wielded. In sermons and discourses, in the generations of commentators that followed them, it was the power of evocation, description, argument, story, and homily that brought the comforting and exacting message of the Rabbis to the Jewish people.

To open a page of the Talmud, of any Rabbinic writing, is to see before one's eyes a pageant of language spanning the centuries. On a single page, side by side, stand columns of Rabbinic texts and commentaries from scholars throughout Jewish history. Below the second-century legal code is the fifth-century commentary and beside that stands the eleventh-century exegete and the seventeenth-century textual scholar. Each contributes something to the spiral of questions, retorts, speculation. Since no words were adequate, the tradition could never stop speaking, and the expanding web of commentary and discourse grew throughout the centuries, as it continues to grow today. All this endless exegesis, this torrent of words, is straining to express that which cannot be adequately said: the secret of what animates the tradition, the consciousness of God in the world, the historical and spiritual experience of millennia. No words can embrace the totality of that message. No rhetoric can soar high enough to scale its peak or burrow deep enough to plumb its depth.

One result of this inability is the potency of silence. As we discussed in chapter 2, silence as a force and even as a prayer is woven throughout the Jewish tradition. The experience of silence as a statement is common enough in our lives as well. When struck by a moment of awesome beauty—the first glance at a masterpiece of man or nature—we are silent. Later, words rush in to fill the void, to explain the experience; but at first we cannot speak. Silence is the mother tongue of awe.

The same experience occurs with a pang of deep love. There are moments when looking at someone will flood a heart, and words seem not only inadequate, but almost a cheapening of the marvel of emotion. Later, when the rush of love subsides, we may be able to mouth the words "I love you." Yet the initial power of the experience is captured only in silence. These are the moments, filled with awe and affection, that the Rabbis and the tradition they shaped shared of God.

One view of the Rabbinic tradition is as a vast, shimmering garment of words wrapped around an inner core of silence. It is the initial moment of silence, of feeling, of rapture, recaptured in the fragile vessel of the word. That is how the Rabbis speak of life and of God.

The outcome of this attitude is the personal nature of Rabbinic portrayals. The words of the Rabbis, attempting to describe the ineffable, are personal, vivid, and at times even outrageous. However bold, the impulse is a mingling of reverence and love. The Rabbis consistently depict God in very intimate terms, in terms of great affection. God is given many names in the Midrash: "Searcher of hearts" (Gen. R. 67:8), "God of consolation" (Ket. 8b), "Beloved" (Song of Songs Rabbah 6:2), "the One who understands" (Pirke Avoth 4:22), and among the most common, simply *Rachmana*—"the merciful One."

BIBLICAL ROOTS
OF THE RABBINIC VIEW

The intimacy of the relationship between human beings and God does not begin with the Rabbis. The Rabbinic relation has a noble pedigree, for it is largely an elaboration of what is already found in many passages in the Bible:

> *O Lord, You have examined me and know me.*
> *When I sit down or stand up You know it.*
> *You observe my walking and reclining,*
> *and are familiar with all my ways. . . .*
> *Where can I escape from Your spirit?*
> *Where can I flee from Your presence?*
> *(Ps. 139:1–2, 7)*

The biblical God is intensely personal, sewn together with anthropomorphic threads. The resultant fabric makes uncomfortable wearing for some who reach for philosophical purity. Precisely what such human description meant to the ancient Israelites, and to the generations that have followed, has been a subject of vast theological and historical investigation. Without treading this complex path, we can say this much: God can be conceived, always has been conceived, in human terms. God is emphatically not a human being, but since we have only human descriptions at our disposal, and have learned to value certain human traits, the Bible delights in fashioning a God who exemplifies the best we can conceive—a God of compassion, of goodness, tenderness, and care.

Even attributes considered negative are routinely ascribed to God: anger, fickleness, severity. For the Rabbis, these were manifestations of God's justice, although this explanation did not always satisfy them. However, they were careful to point out that these attributes should not be emulated. For God, as Rabbi Judah the Prince points out, is master of His anger, whereas anger is the master of human beings (Gen. R. 49:8).

No matter the attribute being discussed, the Talmud informs us that "the Torah speaks in the language of human beings" (Ber. 31b); that is, the biblical descriptions of God are couched in human terms so that we might understand them, not because God is adequately described in that way. So long as such description is understood to be part of human, and not Divine, limitation, we may glory in the insight it brings and the vividness of its depiction of God:

> God is close to those whose hearts are broken. (Ps. 34:19)

> For I know that You are a compassionate and gracious God, slow to anger, abounding in kindness, renouncing punishment. (Jonah 4:2)

> And I will betroth you to Me forever, yea, I will betroth you to Me in righteousness and in justice, in loyalty and in love. And I will betroth you to Me in faithfulness, and you shall know the Lord. (Hosea 2:21)

Yet acknowledging the danger that such descriptions pose—that we might think God is actually a human being—the Bible takes great care to remind us again and again that differences are paramount:

> To whom, then, can you liken Me? To whom can I be compared? —says the Holy One. (Is. 40:25)

> The heavens are the work of Your hands. They shall perish, but You shall endure; they shall all wear out

like a garment. . . . But You are the same, and Your
years never end. (Ps. 102:26–28)

For I am the Lord, I do not change. (Malachi 3:6)

The Bible itself contains both representations of God: He
who is near, and He who dwells in the distant heavens. In
a marvelous verse joining the disparate views, Isaiah pro-
nounces: "For thus said He who high aloft forever dwells,
whose name is holy: 'I dwell on high, in holiness; yet with
the contrite and lowly in spirit—reviving the spirits of the
lowly, reviving the hearts of the contrite' " (Is. 57:15). The
passage containing this verse is chosen for the reading from
the prophets on the Day of Atonement, with its dual theme
of God's Kingship and His compassion. The biblical God is
unutterably majestic and remote. He is also at hand and
caring.

The Rabbinic view of God, in all its splendid and pic-
turesque intimacy, blossoms from such biblical imagery.
The Rabbis did not concoct a God alien to the tradition.
They turned to the God of their ancestors: the God depicted
in so many poetic passages. The God who is, in the Psalmist's urgent words, close to those whose hearts are broken.

Therefore, the Rabbis spoke of God in categories one
would normally reserve for another person: friend, parent,
even lover. Such terms afford an avenue for the expression of
feeling toward God and of relation to Him. Each appellation highlights the part God can play in human life, at
various times and in different situations. One Midrash offers
its own rationale for speaking of God: "We liken God to
His creations in order to understand Him better" (Mechilta,
Bachodesh). Speaking of God in human terms is, in its way,
a religious imperative.

The attitude is summed up in a statement that may
surprise those who assume that, in the Jewish tradition,

legalism is the only path to God. Why should we study the Midrash, the legends and fanciful interpretations of the Rabbis? "If you desire to know He who created this world with words, study the Aggadah [Midrashic legends]" (Sifre Deut. 49). It is through our words that we come to know He who created everything with words. We study the Midrash because through that medium we come to know God.

By examining in turn a few of the personal categories used by the Rabbis to speak of God, a clearer picture will emerge. We shall easily recognize that the unjust caricature of the Pharisaic God as remote, stern, and forbidding is a picture the Rabbis would never have acknowledged as their own or recognized as being an authentic representation of the tradition. Unfortunately, history has often granted those unsympathetic to the Rabbinic idea of God the opportunity to characterize it without correction. The sad result is that even many Jews assume that the misstatements of others are correct, and that their tradition believes in a God of unremitting wrath. Both as an avenue for personal religious exploration and to correct a grievous historical wrong, it is critical to examine the way the Rabbis truly felt about God, a conception that has dominated Jewish thinking ever since.

Friend

God is, in Rabbinic parlance, "the friend of the world" (Hag. 16a). One may speak familiarly to a friend, and there is certainly no lack of familiarity in the address of the Rabbis toward God. In every blessing God is directly addressed: *Baruch atah,* "Blessed are You." That the blessings then shift to third person is a sort of safeguard: it shows we can address God but lest the closeness delude us into thinking we can fathom Him, we move to a more formal mode at the end.

Even with this formality, God is and remains a friend in

the Midrashic mind. In a celebrated example of such direct-
ness (B.M. 59b), God is unceremoniously told to butt out
of a legal discussion the Rabbis are conducting! Rabbi
Eliezer and Rabbi Joshua were engaged in a dispute; after
numerous proofs had been advanced, a voice came out of
heaven and declared that Rabbi Eliezer was in the right.
Rabbi Joshua arose and, quoting Deuteronomy (30:12), declared, "It is not in heaven!" That is, the Torah has been
given to human beings and now they alone have the right to
interpret its provisions. Although this is often used as an
example of human autonomy in legal decision making, it
speaks volumes as well for the Rabbinic attitude toward
God. We can see this from the sequel to the story. Rabbi
Nathan later met the prophet Elijah and asked him: "What
did the Holy One, blessed be He, do when Rabbi Joshua
ignored Him?" "He laughed with joy," replied Elijah, "and
said, 'My children have defeated Me, My children have
defeated Me!' " No more audacious example could be ad-
duced to show how confident the Rabbis were in their sense
of integrity before God, and in their almost collegial relation with Him.

The Rabbinic attitude is not irreverent. Familiarity in
this case breeds not contempt, but devotion. To have a
relationship to God is to understand the awe that God
evokes in the human heart that encounters Him. Reverence
is so highly esteemed that one Rabbinic maxim insists: "All
is in the hands of heaven save the reverence of heaven" (Ber.
33b). God Himself cannot force us to care for Him, to
delight in His ways or His world. But the closer we draw,
the more likely that reverence becomes. Respect for one who
deserves respect is not a function of distance. Proximity to
greatness enhances esteem. To come into relation with the
Ultimate does not diminish devotion, it deepens it.

That God is a friend to all the world appears evident to
the Rabbis. The creation of this universe, with its beautiful

array and potential for sustenance and goodness, was an act of friendship. Friendship is one of the fundamental relations, one of the ways in which human beings must encounter each other if human society is to survive. By generalizing close relationships, we understand how to conduct ourselves with those who are more remote. So unique and important is friendship that God Himself teaches the skill to human beings and creates friendships among people (Pirke de-R.El. 17).

Yet God is more especially the friend of those who care for Him. The Medzibozer Rebbe, a Chasidic leader, went so far as to say: "As one thinks of God in his heart, so does God think of him." God swears eternal friendship to Abraham (Sefer Yetsirah 6:7) and throughout the Bible displays devotion to His faithful. Here again we find a theme common to Rabbinic meditations on God: The quality of the relationship is dependent upon both human beings and God. God cannot, alone and unaided, develop an intimate connection with individuals. The quality and depth of the relationship are finally the choice of the human partner. In the succinct and glowing maxim of the Chasidic Rabbi Menachem Mendle of Kotzk: "Where is God? Wherever human beings let Him in."

This theme, to which we will return, is at the heart of the idea of friendship, which differentiates it from the notion of God as parent. "Parent" does not necessarily define the quality of the relationship. One can be a parent in a tattered and decaying family. The word *parent* alone does not detail the quality of the connection. To be a friend, to be a lover (as we shall shortly see), requires mutuality. God stands in certain relationships to human beings by virtue of His existence and our own. There is no escaping Creator, Parent, Judge. Other relationships depend upon our willingness to give of ourselves, as we do in friendship.

Most important, one can speak to God as one does to a

compatriot, an intimate. To pray, to *davven,* is a kind of Divine conversation. Troubles, imaginings, fears—all come pouring out at the hour of prayer, at any time of the day. There are many reasons to pray: out of need, out of thanks, out of obligation. But there is also the prayer of friendship, of connection to One who knows *machshavot libenu,* the inner workings and aspirations of the human heart. Our souls cry out for communion and understanding. We need someone who knows. Someone who is interested in and hopeful for our lives. Abraham was called the friend of God because he represented God's interests in this world and knew that God cared for him. When he argued for the inhabitants of Sodom, that they be spared, he did not argue as an unworthy subject before an all-powerful ruler: he could challenge God because he stood in relationship to Him.

The Tasks of Friendship   The summation of true friendship is the joined effort of common purpose. Ideally God and humanity work together in this world for betterment and goodness. The ideal of *tikkun olam,* repairing the world, which is critical to the Jewish sense of mission, represents this friendship and partnership between the Divine and human realms. In this part of the relationship there is a certain sublime equality, with God and human beings joined together to purge what is unworthy in this supremely holy enterprise.

Tikkun olam presupposes that the world is "broken" and needs to be fixed by the care and application of people working with the guidance of God. Moral tasks both exalted and everyday, from giving money to one in need to saving a life, are under the inclusive rubric tikkun olam. For each act, no matter the human agent, involves God, if only because He initially pointed the way to mutual care and social justice. In instruction and concern, God participates, as friend of both the doer and the one in need. Together some progress can be made in repairing the world, in making it habitable, in the manner appropriate to a place one must share with a friend.

In each act of decency there is a Divine stake. That is why, in the Talmud, a beggar will solicit money with the curious phrase "acquire merit through me." By giving to those in need, we are credited with merit by God. He has a stake as well.

The human side of friendship with God is predicated upon our legitimate insistence on certain rights; the boundary remains—there can be no friendship of equals—but it is one in which the human side retains its independence and integrity.

Parent

> It is the way of a father to be compassionate and it is the way of a mother to comfort. The Holy One said: "I will act like a father and a mother."
> —Pesikta de-Rav Kahana 19:3

For the Rabbis, God is quintessentially the parent of the human race. This is a recurrent image in the Bible as well. God is the parent and both Israel and the world are frequently called His child. "As a father has compassion for his children," writes the Psalmist, "so the Lord has compassion for those who revere Him" (103:13).

Images of fatherhood emphasize the unity of the human race: "Have we not all one father? Has not one God created us?" (Malachi 2:10). Human beings find ultimate community only in the parenthood of God. For all other bonds— national, social, political, intellectual—may be broken at will. The story of the Tower of Babel is a graphic illustration of how human communities crumble. Despite the presence of a common purpose, the allegory hints at the eternal lesson of human communities: that feuding over goals, egos, and personalities will ultimately tear them apart. The industrious workers who were engaged in "tower building," precisely because they denied the true community of which they *were* a part, the common community of Divine creations, were, in the biblical view, doomed to disintegrate.

Even the most cohesive human groups, with shared interests and histories, do not remain free from bickering and fragmentation. The attempt to replace Divinity with community cannot last, for human associations are finite. There is only one bond among human beings that cannot be destroyed, the bond of being a child of God. It can be betrayed, but never erased. Being God's children means, resolutely and irrevocably, that we are all brothers and sisters.

Like any parent, God frets over the fate of His children, even when they are indifferent to Him: "I responded to those who did not ask, I was at hand to those who did not seek Me; I said, 'Here I am, here I am,' to a nation that did not invoke My name" (Is. 65:1). The quality of Divine concern includes all shades of relation; it takes on that peculiar worry and regard known only to parents.

God is frequently called "father of the world" (M. Prov. 10), a reference not only to His having created ("conceived") the universe, but also to parental concern. God is also a shepherd, the mainstay of the world, and so forth. But the idea of parenting has a particular attraction. It is the parent who pampers the child: "Truly Ephraim is a dear son to Me, a child that is dandled" (Jer. 31:20). God cared for the human race from infancy through adolescence to adulthood. Here the image of mothering is important and apt: "You shall be carried on shoulders and dandled upon knees. As a mother comforts her son, so will I comfort you" (Is. 66:12–13).

A parent is grieved over the misfortunes and mistakes of children, as God is said to be grieved again and again over the stumbling of the human race. A parent wishes and worries; educates and learns; controls gently and must then let go. All of these actions are projected onto the Divine.

The importance of God's portrayal as a parent, and not simply as a King, can be illustrated by a poignant human parallel. In the Bible, Absalom, the son of King David, is estranged from his father. Later, he will rebel against his father and be killed in the attempt to usurp David's throne. But before that, David's agent Joab arranges a last attempt at reconciliation. The incident reads: "Joab went to the king and reported to him; whereupon he summoned Absalom. He came to the king and flung himself face down to the ground before the king. And the king kissed Absalom" (II Sam. 14:33).

The Bible is careful with words, and so we are entitled to notice the designation of David throughout the story: he is always called "king." Never "David," never "father." Knowing as we do that Absalom later rebelled, perhaps we can learn a subtle biblical lesson. Absalom was estranged from his father, and at this last opportunity for healing, David acted not as a father, but as a king. It was the king who kissed Absalom, not the loving father, not the David whom we know from other stories as a sensitive and caring soul. Later, when David grieves for the loss of his son, he might be recalling this moment when pride and position destroyed what remained of a relationship.

God can command *allegiance* because He is a King, but not love. For that, as with human beings, He must be a parent.

The image of parenting is sometimes cited to disparage religious feeling. A more sophisticated approach, it is argued, would recognize that belief in God is, after all, based upon one's early parental yearnings. This is another way of saying that our deepest human emotions are stirred when confronting God, which is true. When the argument is used to prove the *objective* falsity of claims for God, however, it flounders. That we wish God to be a parent does not prove that God must be a purely human projection. We also wish that flowers bloom in color, that children laugh, and that sunsets streak red on the horizon. Not all truths must be painful. Perhaps we do wish God to be a parent. Perhaps God obliges. All human beings can be asked to do is to be honest with their hearts, minds, and souls. We cannot be asked to discard a belief because it comforts us.

The Divine-human relationship is enhanced by the concern and closeness of the "parent-child" relation. We can turn to Yiddish, for example, for the appellation *Tattenu* for God, which is roughly like "our daddy" in English, but with an endearing twist. It is not a repudiation of the awe that is God's due. But awe alone will not shelter nor majesty warm the heart of the fearful. The feeling of God's sheltering presence is bound up in this parent-child relationship. It is in part a relationship of dependence. We know that our lives are fragile, our fortunes various, and we have to depend upon God to preserve us. There is more than simply safety at stake, however; there is giving and love.

All the elements of care, concern, love, and protection that we associate with a caring parent, the Rabbis associate with God. In their desire to demonstrate the inclusiveness of the relationship they parallel all human connections. In one Midrash (Song of Songs Rabbah 3, 2:2) the people are likened to God's daughter and to God's sister. Not content with that, the Midrash has God refer to the people as His mother, thus making God the people's child! The range and variety of relation could not be more dramatic.

In the presence of a loving parent there is a security that time and growth do not diminish. No voice is more reassuring, no love more unconditional and embracing. The tolerance and love of a parent, although sometimes strained, is finally inexhaustible. These are the wondrous attributes that the Rabbis vested in God.

But even the parental imagery is one step below the most direct access. For the Rabbis, drawing upon the Bible, see God in an even more startlingly intimate role—that of a lover.

Lover

God says: "You love Me, and I love you" (M. Ps. 116:1).

In this boldest of anthropomorphic images, God is the lover of the human race. Sometimes the image is one of erotic love, as in the Song of Songs, interpreted by the Rabbis as a love poem between Israel and God. At all times, whatever the particular nuances, the aim is to emphasize that the relation between God and His creations is one of love.

"God loves you." That phrase may strike the modern Jewish ear strangely, but it is authentically and originally a Jewish conception. The love of God for human beings is deep and rich in the Jewish tradition. "I have loved you, says the Lord" is the second verse of the book of Malachi. God's love is expressed again and again in the Bible. It is not the love of a moment, but an everlasting attachment: "The Lord revealed himself to me of old. Eternal love I conceived for you then. Therefore I continue my grace to you" (Jer. 31:3).

The image in Hosea (2:21) of Divine-human betrothal that we noted above is of God's betrothal to Israel. The Rabbis delighted in developing the concept of God's love for humanity in general and for Israel in particular. The love of the Creator is a natural concomitant of creation. God conjured this world out of nothingness because of His love for His creations. The Friday night blessing over the wine informs us that God gave the world the Sabbath, the cornerstone of creation, out of *ahavah v'ratzon*, love and willingness.

This beautiful Rabbinic conception finds liturgical expression in the reciprocal love that shapes the Ahava Rabba and the Shema prayers. Having extolled the beauties of creation, the prayers then personalize the world and its Creator. First the worshiper recites the Ahava Rabba paragraph beginning "With a great love you have loved us, O Lord our God." Immediately following is the first passage of the Shema, which reads: "And you shall love the Lord your God with all your heart, with all your soul, and with all your might." Human beings and God love each other, each according to capacity and kind.

God's love is unconditional, but it is not undiscriminating. The Rabbis understand the verse in Hosea "I will love them freely" (14:5) to mean that God will love us even when we are unworthy, for "free"—i.e., without the certainty of reciprocal love (Tanh. B. Ekeu, 4). Even when humanity fails in its obligations of conduct and decency, it does not forfeit Divine concern. However, there are degrees and differences. God loves all humanity, but can draw closer to those who love Him. For it is those who seek God who have shown their readiness and eagerness for relationship.

More important than the love of God alone is the human awareness of it. Said Rabbi Akiba: "It is with love that God made human beings in His image, but it was with a special love that *He let them know that He made them in His image*" (Pirke Avoth 3:18, emphasis added). To love alone, in secret, is not enough. The benefit to the beloved comes equally from the recognition of love, the feeling of warmth and uniqueness that it bestows. That is a great tragedy of some love, that it exists but is not communicated to the beloved, to the child, the parent, the husband or wife. Even though love abounds, the psychological support is lost. Rabbi Akiba's insight is profound: To be loved is insufficient. The wall of restraint must crumble. Love must be expressed, felt, shared.

IMITATING GOD

We must not imagine that with this description the Midrash reckons that it has captured God. The Rabbis realized that they were not penetrating to God's essence. In the enigmatic words of the Talmud, "God has a special and secret place where He resides and its name is *mistarim*"—mystery (Hag. 5b). There is no access to the ultimate nature and secret of God. Still, God is close enough to describe with encomiums and attributes. Moreover, He is close enough to address. In the wonderful pull of direct relationship, all philosophical caveats fall off and float away like withered leaves.

We can but imagine what it is like to walk through a day in the grip of such intimate communication with God. Behind all, there is God's presence. His nearness is felt. His character is revealed, as far as human understanding permits. God is of the world, constantly seeing, understanding, listening. That is why the Rabbis depict God as the all-seeing eye and all-hearing ear. No thought or wish escapes God's omniscience. "One who knows human thoughts" is yet another, and characteristic, Talmudic designation for God (P. T. San. 1:1). God's watchfulness, not action, is elaborated here. In the seeming absence of activity, there is providential review. Even when the silence was nearly absolute, God observed.

God's watchfulness is but one part of His involvement in human affairs. More important is Divine concern. His is not an indifferent omniscience—He does not know without caring. God's being is suffused with concern, with what A. J. Heschel called "the Divine pathos."

This pathos is more than an abstract quality. Here the specific images of the Rabbis are far more eloquent than any theoretical discussion. They picture a God who is involved in the most intimate way with all of human interpersonal life. God not only helps individuals, He speaks with them, revives their flagging spirits, cares for their woes. God rejoices when human beings are good and laments when they stray. God, in short, is a worrier. In the book of Esther, the Jewish people are threatened with destruction. On the verse "On that night the king's sleep fled" (Esther 6:1), the Rabbis comment: "That night the sleep of the King of Kings [God] fled" (Pirke de-R.El. 50). In this graphic Midrash God (as opposed to the human king, the clear intent of the verse in Esther) is depicted as literally losing sleep over the precarious fate of His people. And this Midrash is not an isolated instance. God is continually described as deeply bound up in the fate of His creations, grieving and exultant, desperate for them to follow His laws and mend their ways.

We are instructed to emulate this combination of qualities: compassion, love, and guidance. *Imitatio Dei* is the Latin term for it, the "imitation" of God. The biblical verse most frequently offered to illustrate this injunction is Leviticus 19:2: "You shall be holy, for I the Lord your God am holy." Human beings are bidden to be like God. Thus one becomes "godlike": Rabbi Levi bar Hama said, "The Holy One, blessed be He, says, 'If you will perform my mitzvot you will become like Me' " (see Deut. R., Lieberman ed., p. xviii).

Human beings are godlike in the Jewish tradition when they act with decency and compassion. They are godlike when they approximate the prophetic ideal of goodness, one that is stern in the grandeur of its vision and still forgiving of the flaws of humanity.

Of course, there are limitations to the extent that we can emulate God. To be godlike is to be distinguished from thinking oneself like God. Even the attempt, however, presupposes that we can know something of God, of His actions, and so of His character. An inaccessible God cannot be imitated. The "Holy One, blessed be He," can be imitated in many ways:

> Said Rabbi Chama b. Chanina: As God clothes the naked ("And the Lord God made garments of skins for Adam and his wife, and clothed them" Gen. 3:21) so must you clothe the naked; as He visits the sick ("The Lord appeared to him [Abraham, after his operation of circumcision] by the terebinths of Mamre" Gen. 18:1) so must you care for the sick; as He comforts the mourners ("After the death of Abraham, God blessed his son Isaac" Gen. 25:11) so must you comfort those who mourn; as He buries the dead ("He [God] buried him [Moses] in the valley in the land of Moab" Deut. 34:6) so must you attend to the burial of the dead. (Sotah 14a)

> "Walking in all His ways" (Deut. 11:22). What are the ways of the Holy One? "A God compassionate and gracious, slow to anger, abounding in kindness and faithfulness, extending kindness to the thousandth generation, forgiving iniquity, transgression and sin . . ." (Ex. 34:6). This means that just as God is gracious and compassionate, you too must be gracious and compassionate. "The Lord is beneficent in all His ways and loving in all his works" (Ps. 145:17). Just as God is beneficent, you too must be beneficent. Just as God is loving, you too must be loving. (Sifre Deut. 49)

The attributes of God are the groundwork upon which morality rests. The Midrash beautifully relates: God is good to all and the greatest good is that His creatures learn from Him to be merciful to one another (Gen. R. 33:3). It is the zenith of human aspiration to imitate God's ways as far as possible and appropriate for a human being. This foundation comes from relationship, from caring, and from love.

The overarching relationship between God and the Jewish people has been codified as a covenant. The covenant, about which so much has been written, is a relationship of love formalized in law. It mandates obligations on both sides. Those obligations are many and complex, and to write a full account of the idea of covenant with its implications would almost be to write a full account of the law and theology of Judaism.

The key is that a covenant is a reciprocal interchange between two partners. One person cannot form a covenant any more than one person can form a friendship. The plank upon which the entire edifice of Judaism is built presupposes a double yearning: human beings for God, and God for human beings. As the Hebrew poet and philosopher Yehuda Halevy wrote: "When I go forth to find You, I find You seeking me."

To know the ways of God and to find ways to God are the passions of the Jewish tradition. The Rabbis do not heap adjectives upon God to diminish, but to magnify. Descriptions and attributions run through their discourse like shimmering jewels, turned over again and again in an exhilarated, profligate rush, the hypnotic effect of dwelling upon the dearly loved. Why would anyone go so far as to speak of God braiding Eve's hair for the wedding with Adam, as the Rabbis did? One appealing answer is that such images reflect the crudity of theological naïveté.

There is another answer. For the Rabbis, these dramatic images were vivid means of expressing the central truth of their lives: the existence of a good and caring God, enmeshed in the trials and triumphs of human life, who looked on them and the world with love. Would an abstract God have been more suitable? Perhaps, if our principal concern were that the Rabbis accommodate us by adopting our theological presumptions. We may discover, however, that there is a greater wisdom in the supposed "elementary" theology of the Rabbis than there is in the more elaborate constructs of the scholastics. Images of God as parent, friend, lover, among many others, are the only ways in which human beings can express the intensity and immediacy of relationship. The religious and human vitality of these depictions can be blanched and scoured by a refined intellectualism. Or they can stand as the theological poetry that has shaped the Jewish tradition for two thousand years.

In the preceding chapter we spoke about the death of Moses. In this chapter, it is fitting to close with the beginning of the relationship between God and Moses, particularly because it is so pertinent to our theme.

Before Moses was called to be a leader, he was a shepherd for his father-in-law, Jethro. One day while pasturing his flock, he saw the burning bush. The biblical text is precisely phrased: "He gazed, and there was a bush all aflame, yet the bush was not consumed. Moses said, 'I must turn aside to look at this marvelous sight; why doesn't the bush burn up?' *When the Lord saw that he had turned aside to look, God called to him out of the bush:* 'Moses! Moses!' " (Ex. 3:2–4, emphasis added).

God did not speak to Moses until Moses demonstrated that he was caring enough, observant enough, alive enough to the wonders of this world to turn aside and see them. Others, assert the Rabbis, had passed this bush before; only Moses noticed the miracle.

And what was the image of God projected to Moses as a result? God, said the Rabbis, did not call out Moses' name in a thundering voice. Rather, He spoke with the voice of Moses' father. When Moses answered, thinking his own father was speaking, God replied, "No, Moses, I am not your father, but the God of your father. I spoke this way because I did not wish to frighten you." Then God proceeded to tell Moses of his daunting mission (Ex. R. 3:1).

God in this legend notices the slight but significant merits of His creations. His tenderness is clear. So careful is He of Moses' feelings that He does not wish to frighten him, or impress him with grandeur. All the themes— parent, friend, and lover—are bound up in this simple declaration: "I am . . . the God of your father. I spoke this way because I did not wish to frighten you." With that began the closest relationship between God and an individual human being known to the Bible.

Images themselves, however beautiful, are not forces for religious feeling unless they are reflective of some deeper perspective out of which they grow. And indeed from the images of the Rabbis, from their words and works, we can discover a certain kind of worldview, a deeper sense of their outlook. Out of the discussions we have recounted in this chapter, and a great deal more, there emerges a certain cast of mind, one that we examine in the following chapter.

5

Normal Mysticism

A woman once asked Rabbi Jose ben Halafta: "If creation
was completed in only six days, what has God been doing
since?" He answered: "God spends His time building lad-
ders, for some to ascend, and others to descend."
—Leviticus Rabbah 8:1

Ideas are not incidental to character. What we are is largely
a product of how we see the world, and when our views
mature or change, our demeanor and daily behavior change
with them. To deal in ideas is to touch the heart of human
conduct. We are not only what we do, but what we think,
although those thoughts may lie hidden from ourselves.

In many ways Judaism views action as primary; it is the
only tangible measure of a person or society. Yet the interplay of idea and action is far from clear. Is what we think a
product of the experience we have? Or is the opposite the
case—is our behavior dependent upon the concepts we hold
dear?

On the one hand there exists a wise Rabbinic principle,
mitoch sheloh lishmah bah lishma: one should perform the
proper action even if it is done without proper intention,
because the intention will follow. We know that people can
be educated through action to elevate their intentions. Any
athlete will attest that in a game or sport the love of it and
the knowledge of it grow with practice. The only way to
learn the game is to play the game. This is the side of

Judaism that sees the act as primary. Doing good takes precedence over proper thinking, since action has an immediate effect. No matter how exalted one's concept of justice, it is only by practicing justice, by doing just acts, that the world will be made better.

Still, in some ways the idea, the "proper thinking," is sovereign. No single action can encompass the notion of liberty or justice, and it is the abstract ideal that often determines how one looks at life, and so how one acts. We hold to certain notions of what it means to be good, or kind, and those abstract notions help guide us through our lives. For the Rabbis, the concept of God was the lodestar, the shining idea by which streams of daily life were navigated.

In a fascinating Talmudic dispute (Kidd. 40b), the Rabbis try to decide whether study or practice should claim priority. Is it more important to be expert in what God asks of human beings or to practice, even without certain knowledge of the proper path? Finally they decide that study is more important than action, *because study leads to proper action.* Study alone is worthless, for it will not make a whit of difference to the world if one is educated or boorish unless such knowledge alters behavior. Conversely, simply to act has no value. We would doubtless prefer that the arsonist not act. To act appropriately is the goal, and for that, attitudes must be educated.

Up to this point we have been exploring the Rabbinic idea of God. In this chapter and the next our concern will be to trace the influence of that concept on the worldview of the Rabbis and their systems of action. In each part of the discussion we are seeking to understand how these attitudes and behaviors might enrich our own lives. We study the ancient discussions of the Rabbis in part to help guide us today. Perhaps we can learn from their outlook how to address some of the deeper dilemmas that bedevil the modern soul.

THE RABBINIC OUTLOOK

How did the Talmudic Rabbis, and their spiritual descendants throughout the ages, look at life? Is there a shortcut to understanding how they communicated their approach to others, and to God?

Some fifty years ago, the scholar Max Kadushin coined a curious term to describe the Rabbis of the Talmud and Midrash. He called them "normal mystics." The paradox in the words is deliberate. We do not think of mystics as everyday people. The word evokes an aura of otherworldly apparitions. As Kadushin pointed out, the unadorned term "mystic" does not apply to the Rabbis.

A *normal* mystic does not have hallucinatory visions of celestial glories. A normal mystic does not spend days and nights in ascetic pursuits, conjuring up some other, arcane realm of existence. A normal mystic is not a cave-dwelling Corybant practicing secret rituals. He is normal.

Still the tag "mystic" remains. For a normal mystic is one who sees—or, better, feels—the shaping and guiding hand of Divinity in all things. No event, whether personal, political, or natural, is outside the realm of Divine providential concern. The normal mystic is, in the phrase often used to describe the philosopher Spinoza, God-intoxicated. Drunk with the Divine. An awareness of God seeps into all the activities of human life until this unseen presence is taken as the true ground of being, more real than what we glibly dub "reality."

Normal mysticism was the outlook that shaped the Rabbinic tradition mandating that a blessing be recited for all manner of things: a beautiful sight in nature, an earthquake, a rainbow, a scholar, a potentate, a meal. The great range of experience was related to its origins in the Divine. No natural or human eminence could pass by without the Rabbis acknowledging the presence and grace of Divinity behind it. Without God the mountains would not be raised, nor the sea roar. There would be no bread on the table. There would be no governments, societies, glory. There would be no wisdom or wonder. There would be no life. The normal mystic is the exceptional individual who is ever conscious of what is taken to be a pervasive albeit elementary truth: God's presence and providence are everywhere.

Perhaps we can explain the difference between the mystic and the normal mystic by suggesting that they reach the same place by different routes. Each seeks God. The mystic tries to find God by absenting himself from his fellow human beings, because they are a distraction from the single-minded pursuit of God. By trying to leave the world behind, the mystic seeks to discover its true foundation.

The normal mystic, on the other hand, plunges *into* the world to uncover its foundation. In the eyes of another human being, in the daily activity of average people, the normal mystic seeks the presence of God. Not the telescope but the microscope, is the proper scientific analogue: the normal mystic is the searcher for the wonder near at hand. The normal mystic looks at life as you and I know it, but with an acute eye, one that tracks the almost imperceptible or often overlooked suggestion of God in every corner, at each turn.

From this awareness arises the unshakable conviction of wholeness and artistry woven throughout the earth. What we are describing is a posture more emotive than analytic. Recall the Midrash cited previously: God is more than the Creator. He is the ultimate Artist, and so the proper way to view creation is as a superlative work of art.

A normal mystic does appreciate the world as a work of art, and sees its flaws as not only moral but also as artistic lapses. This is no dilettantish attitude: seeing life as a canvas and human options as the palette from which we must paint our fates is a serious and weighty view. For to create a work of art out of existence is not solely an aesthetic task. Morality and reverence are the working tools for the competent artist of life. Goodness, decency, learning—all these and more color the canvas of our years.

The prototypical artist in the Jewish tradition was Bezalel ben Uri. He was the individual designated by God in the Bible to fashion the tabernacle. Significantly, this great artist was engaged in constructing something for God. It was not a statue for the glorification of the human being, as was the practice in other civilizations. Human artistry was and is a tribute to Divine artistry.

This is a different attitude toward the nature and purpose of art. In our time art's primary motivation is the exaltation of the artist, or of the ideal "Art" or, perhaps, the edification of the community. Ultimately we do not share the assumption of the biblical artist, that art exists to serve God; that humanly created beauty is a tribute to the Divine creation.

Unfortunately, beauty is often pressed into the service of moral frivolousness or worse. The worship of art for its own sake is a dangerous and amoral attitude. We are regularly seduced by the undeniable power of art into assuming it to be good, as opposed to simply beautiful or moving. Art alone is not to be worshiped, for that is merely another form of idolatry. On the other hand, the creation of beauty should not be disregarded or derided, for art can be a noble and enduring human achievement. We need a deeper perspective on the place of the symphony, the canvas, the poem: they are enormously important to human life, but they are not the transcendent ideal we seek.

There is beauty of a similar kind, aesthetic and artistic beauty, in a life sparked by moral concerns. Self-sacrifice, generosity, justice, and a thousand other concepts and acts that constitute our moral life are also aesthetically powerful and touching. The beauty in a well-lived life is not inferior to that of a well-written novel: it is merely more difficult, more sustained, more accessible to different temperaments and talents, and ultimately more important.

We have shifted ground, from the world as a work of art to human life as art. The shift is deliberate, for the two are not easily separable. The Rabbinic vision delights in and dwells upon the unity of all things, and human life cannot be isolated from the earthly stage upon which it is played. We are part of all that is, an integrated whole fashioned by the hand of the Artist. The artistry of life, part of the human task, is tied to stewardship of this planet with which we were presented. The Talmud considers human beings partners in creation. Artistry is not God's alone.

THE PERSONAL GOD
OF THE NORMAL MYSTIC

The normal mystic is not a seeker after an abstract and distant God. Personalization is inescapable. God's constancy behind the pageant of the universe can be seen only if one has an image of the personality of God. The believer, knowing God, detects God's presence in His creation. Not so different is the way we acquaint ourselves with the home of a friend. The better the friend is known, the more one realizes, even in his or her absence, that this must be the friend's house. The paintings are to his taste, the furnishings reflect her balance between comfort, economy, and aesthetics. The piano and chess set reflect his pursuits. Each detail whispers the personality of the owner. An item that to the uninitiated would say nothing, speaks eloquently to one who knows the owner's character, likes and dislikes, talents, tastes.

The analogy is imperfect, of course, because God cannot be as accessible and tangible as another person. But the eye attuned to the Divine finds the stamp of God impressed upon the world in everyday sights and events. God can be seen in this world because one knows what sort of God has fashioned it. The creation reflects the persona of the creator. "My children," said Rabbi Akiba to his disciples, "just as the existence of a house testifies to the builder, the garment to the weaver, and the door to the carpenter, so does the world testify to the Holy One, blessed be He, who created it" (Midrash T'murah).

Philosophically, such blatant personalization is thoroughly unacceptable. You cannot decide upon God's personality and then claim to have found it lurking in lakes and trees. To a Midrashic mind, on the contrary, it is not only acceptable, but necessary. How else can one be true to one's earthly experience, in which everything is reminiscent of God? To the worshiper all of creation speaks of God: the cliffs proclaim His majesty, the human mind His subtlety and fidelity, the vast panoply of the cosmos His power and intimate concern together.

The normal mystic feels God in an acute way. What is to others the mute order of nature, to him or her is the constant blaring testimony of God's presence in the world. "The heavens declare the glory of God," writes the Psalmist (19:1), and in that declaration is a certainty nearly incomprehensible to one not sharing the Psalmist's sharpened sense of the Divine in life. Indeed, the possibility that others will not see God in the heavens is assumed by the continuation of the Psalm: "there is no speech, there are no words, their voice is not heard" (19:3). This is a poetic vision, and poetry is often a private affair. Here, however, the subject is the Author of the universe, and the stake no less than the sum of human destiny. Therefore, it has long been the design of Scripture and interpretation to coax others into sensing God's presence. A great deal of religious writing is the artist's attempt to evoke in his listener the vision that dances behind his own eyes.

The constant consciousness of God's presence. There is no more succinct way to summarize the Rabbinic model.

This is not meant as a scholarly evaluation of the outlook of the Rabbis. In fact, for our purposes Kadushin's term is most valuable when generalized to describe not the Rabbinic mind, but the religious Jewish mind as it has developed over millennia. Normal mysticism has been a component of Judaism from the first, from the sublime ancient panegyrics of the prophets through the medieval poets to the groping hesitancy of the moderns. In moments of greater grace, the believing Jew has found this world shot through with the glory of God.

Such a pervasive consciousness is found implicitly and overtly in the Bible. Many readers have noticed that the biblical book of Esther, as an example, contains no mention of God's name. Yet in the almost miraculous deliverance of the people, God's presence is keenly felt. In the comeuppance of Haman is God's justice, in the salvation of Esther and Mordecai, and ultimately the entire people, God's compassion. The artistry of the book is to insinuate God's providence even when it cannot be directly "seen." God's name may not be found in the book, but His presence suffuses the story, and that is the lesson the author of this tale would have us read in the world as well.

Whatever the historical circumstance in which this subtle silence was fashioned, it reflects the normal mystical theme. God is present in the artist's design throughout the scroll of Esther although His presence is merely suggested. The tale allows the reader to "play" normal mystic by seeing God in the occurrences of everyday life and history, as the Rabbis did. As in life, God does not miraculously step upon the stage to usher in the denouement in the manner of a celestial cavalry. Rather, the suggestion emerges slowly, subtly. As if one had dipped the sturdy white sheet into photographic solution, the providential image gradually appears, the picture sharpens, until at last one marvels that it ever seemed hidden at all.

Genesis provides a still older example of hidden and revealed divinity in the story of Joseph and his brothers. Here too, events are pushed along in a remarkably providential manner without direct mention of God. Joseph is sent by his father to seek out his brothers, but he does not know where they have gone. In searching for them he comes across a helpful stranger. Designated in the text only as "a man," he informs Joseph that his brothers have gone on to Dothan (37:15–17). This man was traditionally taken to be an angel, and for good reason. His appearance (and his knowledge of the brothers' whereabouts) was too serendipitous to be a true coincidence. This must be the hand of God. At the very end of the narrative, Joseph insists to his bewildered and frightened brothers that it was God, and not they (who had earlier sold him into slavery), who orchestrated the entire episode: "Now do not blame yourselves or be angry that you sold me here—for God sent me to save lives" (45:5). The careful reader has been primed, and knows that Joseph is telling the truth.

THE GOD OF HISTORY

Stories in which God makes an indirect appearance lead us to the wider field of the normal mystical vision. The story of Esther is not a personal redemptive tale; it purports to be a historical chronicle. The Jews of Shushan are saved, in the kind of national miracle for which the Jews would so often yearn. The normal mystical vision embraces history along with nature.

The sense of being in the march of events, part of an

immemorial parade through the centuries, is as tangible a part of the vision of coherence and ultimate mystery as is the beauty of nature.

The modern Jewish philosopher Emil Fackenheim has argued that God appears only to specific people in specific situations. That may be, but in the Jewish tradition those appearances can be historically decisive. Jewish history saw in the ultimate redemption a process guided by the hand of God. God's personality was not only addressed to the individual—it was addressed to collective humanity. It spoke through history. However much we concentrate in the present discussion on the individual quest for God, it should not blind us to the tremendous role in Jewish thought and life of the God of history and collectivity.

Those same patterns that emerged in the natural order were seen by the Rabbis in the affairs of humanity as well. There were cycles of enslavement and redemption. History had periods of triumph and disaster. Through it all, even though history was fashioned by human beings, God was visible. In the end, when there would finally be peace, the unraveled skeins of human history would be brought together, and the patterns become clear.

Obviously this is a more difficult aspect of God to accept than the purely individual God. Does God indeed act through history? Are not the tides of war and destruction enough to convince us that history marches apace without Divine guidance, and certainly without Divine intervention?

Without entering the question of evil in the world for the moment (see chapter 8), we may note that for God to be in history does not mean that God directs all events. Rather, in the normal mystical vision God's presence may be in the slight nudging of the process, the murmured word in a human ear that can direct a life in the service of humanity. Perhaps God can sometimes inspire, if not force. Whatever we may make of it, God is certainly viewed, in the normal mystical estimation, as taking a part in history. For it is not only in the rising of the sun and the budding of a flower that God is seen. He is seen in the critical area of human action.

The Bible is a reading of history with God directing almost all the action. While such extravagant control is far beyond what a modern reader can accept or desires, it does not mean that everything under the sun is solely of human contrivance. Perhaps God, in some gentle, unobtrusive way, whispers His wish to the human experience.

DOUBLE VISION: POTENTIALITY

The English essayist Hazlitt wrote: "Man is the only animal that both laughs and cries, for he is the only animal struck by the difference between what is and what should be." Normal mysticism involves just this double vision—life as it is, and as it was intended to be. The vast legal/ethical system of the Rabbis is an expression of an immense, insistent vision: life as it is is unacceptable, and it is the human mission always to strain at the seams, seeking change.

In contrast to our usual image of the mystic as a distant hermit, the normal mystic is more *in* this world than most. For to be truly sensitive to the world is to be constantly aware of emerging patterns. As Rabbi Shimon said, the characteristic of wisdom is "to be able to envision the consequences of one's actions" (Pirke Avoth 2:13). To see things as they are being born is the true intuitive trick of wisdom. Evaluating existence solely on the basis of its present state is unproductive, even unrealistic: it will change, and unless one can understand its direction and possibilities, it will change without the guidance of vision. But when existence is viewed against the backdrop of possibility, keeping constantly in mind what *might* be, the normal mystic can evaluate what is without losing sight of the animating force behind the world, without falling into the common and critical mistake of assuming that what is must be.

The perception of human nature as an irreplaceable spark of the Divine does not allow one to escape the way people truly are. The betrayal of human dignity is more painful and lamentable if one has a vision of what human beings might be. Ugliness is most awful to an eye practiced in viewing beauty.

The prophets and sages of Israel frequently seemed harsh in their condemnations of apparently trivial misdeeds. (Which is not to say that monstrous offenses were not also condemned.) This harshness is a tribute. The assumption of human excellence brings impatience with human degradation. If we are, in the Psalmist's words, created just lower than angels (Ps. 8:6), then the barbarism of human beings becomes more revolting, more difficult to endure. A believer's eyes are not unfocused, the gaze is not naive. They are simply conditioned by looking at potential in contrast to things as they now stand. Their judgment depends upon that most difficult of evocations, the power to conjure up a world that is both better and still within human possibility. It is a difficult but essential balancing act to be hopeful without being utopian. For the religious mind is constantly aware that perfection does not belong to human beings, and that history has been blackened by the inhumanity of those who would accept only what they styled a perfect society.

Heschel once described a prophet as one capable of holding God and humanity in his mind simultaneously. Without controverting this definition, we might expand it to include another duality: the normal mystic is capable of holding the present, in all its particularity and ambivalence, in mind simultaneously with the future the present might become. In short, the normal mystic is a genius of potentiality.

There is this commonality between the prophet and the normal mystic. It is often mistakenly assumed that the true function of a prophet was to tell the future. Actually, prophets were seers who told of the present. One who sees deeply enough into the present will understand the unfolding of events and so know something of the future. The insight, however, is not a magical foretelling of things to come, but a penetrating understanding of things that are. Peering into the future is a skill of those who see the potential of the present.

Seeing potential in life can be illustrated by a classic instance from the arts. A viewer of Michelangelo's statue *David* cannot help but be struck by its setting. The hall leading to the *David* is lined with "emerging slaves," sculptures that are more or less realized, coming out of the roughly hewn rock. Some are barely visible, others almost completely emerged. Each is in a different state of freedom from the rock that gave birth to it and yet still holds it. At the end of the hall looms the *David,* perfectly formed, standing as though it had always been there, as if it had never been merely a rough block of unshaped stone. The awed visitor then turns back and looks at those first few undefined hunks of rock to wonder how Michelangelo could have envisioned his masterpiece hiding in the uncut stone. The answer lies in the possibility of seeing potential. The genius of moral artistry is to see possibilities of goodness, of beauty, even when all is ugliness and evil. To believe, however impossible it seems, in the latent beauty behind the blank, bleak material in which that beauty is entombed.

There is a legend in the Talmud concerning the education of a great scholar, Resh Lakish, that makes the same point. Resh Lakish, we are told, began life as a bandit. One day he happened upon Rabbi Jochanan, whose discerning eye caught something special in the young man. Rabbi Jochanan insisted that someone with Resh Lakish's vigor and strength should turn toward nobler pursuits. In time, Resh Lakish became a prominent sage because someone had been able to see not only what was, but the possibilities inherent and unrealized in this unusual man (B.M. 84a).

The Bible is filled with tales of those whose potentials were suddenly recognized: Abraham, Rebekah, Moses. For to see a *David* in a blank block of stone, to see Resh Lakish in a bandit, to see Moses in a shepherd—all these are great acts of constancy and of faith. All suggest the wisdom of the normal mystic.

A DIFFERENT HERO

It is an easy cliché of modern society that we have no heroes, or too few heroes. In truth we have too many. Figures of idealization are thrown at us through sports, movies, television, at a dizzying clip. Adoration of talent, wealth, or of that dangerous imponderable "charisma" is rife in our culture. Paradoxically, this proliferation of heroes has created not a glut, but a lack. There are few true models of heroism to emulate, and those few are often ignored. The Jewish tradition has, in the normal mystic, a special kind of hero, a genuine hero who is worth notice.

For a "hero" in the Jewish tradition is first defined by morality and adherence to the principles of God. Without decency, no amount of talent, energy, or even genius can make one a hero. After the difficulties and defeats of the plagues, doubtless many Egyptians considered Pharaoh's pursuit of the Israelites into the wilderness an act of consummate heroism. It took great courage to buck the apparently supernatural forces fighting on the opponent's side. In casting off the timidity that is a natural result of repeated disaster, Pharaoh demonstrated remarkable, if foolish, bravado. But courage is a quality in the service of ends, and if the ends be immoral, the courage is no salvation. Pharaoh was no hero. The Israelites who had to step into a parted Red Sea, an act of infinitely less courage because born of desperation, were heroes, for their actions were in the service of freedom, and of God.

Heroism in the normal mystical vein is a function of vision, a conviction about action, an attempt to move this intractable sphere into conformity with what it should be without obliterating differences. Heroism is everyday heroism too, performed by those whose talents are used to better human life. Though perhaps lacking in drama, in the excitement and brio that surround more celebrated "heroes," authentic heroism is often a sedate affair: the heroism of one who cares for someone who is sick, feeds another who is hungry, decides to take time to perform some small act of goodness.

Why did God choose Moses to be the leader of Israel? We have already noted one explanation, which credited Moses' powers of alertness and observation: that he turned aside to look at the burning bush. But what made God decide that Moses was a worthy candidate to test for leadership?

The Midrash tells the following tale: When Moses was tending his father-in-law's flock, a young sheep escaped from him. He pursued it for a long time, finally catching up with the sheep as it drank from a pool of water. Moses waited until it had finished drinking and said: "I did not know you ran away because you were thirsty. You must be weary." So he lifted the young animal up onto his shoulders and carried it back to the flock. When God saw how merciful he was with this little sheep, He knew Moses would be kind to Israel. Because, the Midrash states, when God wishes to test people's character, He looks at the way they tend sheep (Ex. R. 2:2).

Moses became the leader of Israel not because of any

dramatic, heroic act, but because of a small kindness, a bit of everyday heroism. How we treat the weak and needy is the measure of our heroism. For each of us, the question is not what dragons we have slain, but how we tend sheep.

The normal mystic in the Jewish tradition was one whose life was devoted to the "repairing imperative," that things must be mended, a sense livened by the constant perception of God's presence and concern behind all things. Acting on that perception makes one a hero.

LEGALISM AND
NORMAL MYSTICISM

A mystic in any sense may seem far removed from the stringent legalism that many consider characteristic of Judaism. The apparent difference fades when we recall that a worldview is consequential only if it makes changes in the everyday action of its adherents. To see the hand of God and yet leave one's daily life unaffected by that perception is the greatest blasphemy. To deny is not so grievous as to ignore.

Part of the intent of ritual is to foster a link through the generations, and so a sense of the great, if hidden, historical presence behind all action. Moreover, a system of law knits the society together and fosters just that advance which is the normal mystic's dearest vision. We will discuss ritual in greater detail in the next chapter. We can already see, however, that in Judaism law became the everyday expression of the exalted perceptions of prophets and visionaries. Normal mysticism and legalism are kin, not contraries. The drive to act so as to reflect love of God is a powerful one, and ritual enables the believer to give specific expression to the tremendous forces swelling in his or her soul. The scholar and rabbi Solomon Schechter once sagely observed that "man cannot live on oxygen alone." We cannot survive on sublime ideas alone. They must be translated into life, brought to the marketplace and the home, to the synagogue, to the community as well as to the solitary moment of reflection. Normal mysticism in Judaism is distinguished by remaining more than an attitude—it becomes a way of life. The skeleton of spiritualism is clothed by action, ritual, tradition, precept—all the accoutrements of a vital religious faith. For without specific prescriptions, no worldview can be transmitted from one generation to the next. Attitudes are not acquired by osmosis but by action, explanation, and modeling. As the story has it, one fervent disciple traveled for days to see not how his master studied or taught, but how he tied his shoes. For each action, however humble, can reflect the sanctity of the person.

Normal mysticism is partly a name for several different phenomena with which we are already familiar. A drive to goodness is part of it, as is the ability to find beauty in the natural world and in the actions of human life. None of this is a new approach, although the connection between the two is not always apparent. What ties the perspective together, however, is that it all revolves around an acute awareness of God's presence in all things at all times. This is the heart of the normal mystical conception. Where another sees only an act of charity, the normal mystic sees the idea of Divinity playing at the edges, spurring an individual on to do what is apparently contrary to his own interest, in the interest of another. Where another sees an "average" human being, the normal mystic sees a coiled spring of human potential for goodness, for transcendent action, a creature of infinite worth, a being loved by God. Where another sees the prescribed ritual, the external action, the normal mystic feels the rich conceptual background, the way in which the simplest act can speak eloquently of man's place in this world.

Once when the great sage Hillel had completed his teaching, his disciples asked him where he was going. "To perform a religious obligation," he said. "Which obligation?" they asked. "I am going to bathe," he answered (Lev. R. 34:3). He then explained to his students that the care of the human body, this gift of God, is also a religious obligation. This speaks not only of the Rabbi's healthy sense of the body, but of the elevation of everything in life to a level of sanctity. The simple daily care we take of ourselves, the normal routine and duties that fill our days—all of these are occasions for the celebration of spirit. Religion should not be confined to the moment set aside for ritual function. It pervades each instant of life.

Of course, this sense does not simply happen and it does not happen simply. To become more alive to the higher reaches of ourselves requires effort, even training. The Rabbinic tradition sought to train people by regulating its perception of God so that it could be shared.

This chapter has come full circle, ending with the opening theme of the complicated interplay of attitude and action. There can be no definitive answer to the relation between them, but this much seems certain: both are tightly textured in human character, and both must be addressed. Text, homily, story, interpretation, dispute—all this and more aim at the ideas and attitudes of the listener. Certain prescribed actions are essential to solidify such ideas, just as the ideas help animate the behavior. We will now examine the ways in which Judaism seeks to create "normal mystics" by teaching us how to "speak" spiritual language.

6

Spiritual Language

I love to know that the Lord listens to my supplication.
—Psalms 116:1

Communication. The word dominates much of our discourse yet its absence is one of our most intractable problems. Masters of range and simultaneity, we have lost a special dimension to language. The very commonness of certain types of communication, the ease with which a voice is flung over continents and images are projected worldwide, has led to a decline of communication that is more difficult and demanding. Electronic information abounds, but the capacity to wrench feelings from the heart and share them suffers. Struggling to speak is a less urgent impulse when we are so often and entertainingly spoken to. Conversation declines as television instructs us in human language as a facile but limited tool, more suited to entertain than to touch.

Human life demands deep speaking, demands interchanges on levels that casual conversation cannot approach. That need is sabotaged by the incessant airing of chatter and prattle. As a society we must relearn the possibilities of profound dialogue. A Hebrew epigram teaches that words that come from the heart enter the heart. After the wizardry of modern communications, with the astonishing facility we have developed in transmission, comes the relearning of skills long neglected, those of speaking from the heart.

This chapter is concerned with a unique language, one related to but not identical with speech. There is no precise parallel upon which to draw. We tend to assume communication is essentially the art of speaking and of visual presentation. The audience is usually apparent, measurable, similar in kind and concern to the communicator. The language that engages us here is of another sort altogether: this language seeks to guide one in opening and sustaining a dialogue with God.

That dialogue is cumulative, for mutual understanding is a progressive skill. We speak to a friend of thirty years differently than to an acquaintance of thirty minutes. There is a pool of shared association, experience, a shorthand of language that creeps into the discourse of lovers or friends. This does not arise overnight. It must be cared for, lovingly cultivated, tended and kept fresh. So it is with God.

In certain special times it is possible to find the joy of instant, intense rapport with another. Strangers may discover that, precisely because of the lack of connection, it is easier to talk to each other than to intimates. One's deepest thoughts can be bared without having to face the person again the next day with the knowledge that one's inner soul has been shared and is known. This sort of immediate contact too can be found with God, although obviously God will not be "gone" the next day. Yet such fortuitous connections tend to rust or fade if not tended. Prescribed forms and regular effort are essential if that marvelous rapport is to remain and grow.

Human dealings of every variety demand certain skills. In the Jewish tradition, the Divine-human discourse takes place within definite frameworks that one needs to learn.

Jewish tradition at its best is a continuing conversation, as between friends, or lovers. There are shared ideas, experiences, even shorthand remarks that cannot be understood by those outside the relationship. Each conversation draws upon volumes of joint realizations and understandings. The past is never discarded in the fullness of a loving relationship. At the same time, it is always certain that there is more to say. Those who relate to God as though merely exploring what has already been said are missing the critical play of innovation and newness that can keep even the oldest associations vital. According to the Jewish tradition, people are forever engaged in dialogue with God, and there is always more to add.

Even without a detailed description of the language or structure of Jewish practice, we can isolate certain themes in the Jewish ritual structure that allow us a way into this centuries-old dialogue. Given the idea of God that the Rabbis have bequeathed to us, our task is, quite simply, to open the conversation.

PRAYER

The Rabbis call prayer "the service of the heart." The sacrificial metaphor (for "service" in the phrase above recalls the service and sacrifices of the Temple) is suggestive. Jewish prayer is built upon the idea that an offering is being made to God. Something is being given—the fervor and fullness of our souls. "One's prayer is not heeded," says the Talmud, "unless God is approached with one's heart in one's hands" (Taanit 8a).

Prayer is the complete act of the human spirit, touching all the faculties—intellectual, emotional, spiritual, and even physical (in the prescribed motions of prayer). Such an offering is intended to be complete, the worshipers placing themselves on a metaphorical altar, putting themselves "on the line" in the hopes of acceptance.

One difference between prayer and human communication is the assurance of God's acceptance, if not God's assent. The tradition accepts that God will embrace any prayer that is offered willingly and fervently.

This does not make prayer easy. For if the assurance of acceptance is one difference between human and Divine communication, the other difference is the uncertainty of response. We cannot know if anyone is listening. Is prayer truly a dialogue, or only a monologue? Any response in our lives to prayer is erratic at best. At times it is tempting to believe that something has been granted in answer to our request. In more sober moments we realize, however, that prayers do not appear to be answered in this world, that far too much is faithfully asked for and not given. If what we ask for is not granted, can we still maintain there is "response"?

Only inside can we feel if there is any reply. No activity in the world can conclusively demonstrate dialogue. Perhaps in the subjective chambers of the individual soul one may conclude that there was communication, but it is highly personal and ever uncertain. Everyone who prays struggles with the deep fear that this time, the only answer will be absence, silence.

The uncertainty of an answer is not the only obstacle to prayer. Even in more positive moments, when one is feeling the assurance of God's acceptance, to present oneself fully to God is extraordinarily difficult. We know the enormous resistance that wells up inside us when we seek to open ourselves to another human being. Fear rises like a wall in the soul and fights to keep us locked in and safe. That same wall rises when we seek to pray. At times it looms larger, since to open oneself to God entails greater surrender, even less certainty.

Nonetheless, the proclamation of God's compassionate acceptance is the sturdy undercurrent of Jewish prayer: "A broken and contrite heart, O Lord, You will not despise," cries the Psalmist (51:19). In the course of Jewish history, endless meditations, exercises, detailed programs, and recitations have been developed for prayer, with many still in use, more long since discarded. They were never intended to reflect the emptiness of certain legislated phrases or the seemingly impressive recitation of long memorized prayers. Rather they have all been aimed ultimately at one state of mind: the worshiper should feel the impact of his or her action and should be willing to offer up a soul to God.

Maintaining fervor in any activity is a challenge. In prayer, when immediate rewards are often not apparent, it is particularly demanding. The discipline of regular prayer is difficult enough, with the pressing obligations of every day wearing down resolve. Yet the true obstacle to prayer is not its regularity but its depth. In the Talmud we are told that God requires the heart (San. 106b). To offer a heart in prayer is to open oneself, peeling off the rugged armor with which we shield our souls in a hostile world. It means abandoning our need for certainty in interaction, and allowing ourselves to be swept up in a dialogue as ancient as it is powerful. Learning, in short, how to speak with God.

Although there is an incantational aspect to prayer, Jewish prayer is not empty of content. The Jewish prayer service is more than a mantra. All prayer has a message, addressed to the worshiper as well as to God. There is a story told of a man who once approached his Rabbi and said: "You know, Rabbi, I do not mean to boast, but I consider myself quite a learned man. I have been through the entire Talmud three times." The Rabbi smiled, nodded, and said, "That is admirable, my friend. But tell me, how much of the Talmud has been through you?" Similarly, the ideal is not only to go through the prayers, but to have the words, the meaning, the message, filter through us.

What we choose to pray reflects our conception of ourselves and the human mission as well as our ideas about the Author of the universe. A brief glance at one or two examples will acquaint us with some priorities of prayer in the Jewish tradition.

At the beginning of the morning service is a series of simple yet devastating questions: "What are we? What is our life? What is our goodness? What is our righteousness? What is our help? What is our strength? What is our might? What can we say before You, O God?" These questions are intended to strip the easy façade of self away, and force the receptive reader to face central concerns. They lead carefully in concentric, widening circles. First they ask us to consider: What is your foundation as a person? How is it that you are here? Then they proceed to our actions toward others who are here, our righteousness and goodness. And finally, to the basis of our strength and help, He who created us. Conscious now of the disparity between the promise of the human being in the first question and the actual conduct of our lives, we ask what self-justifying plea we could possibly offer. The questions highlight our inadequacies and our virtues and force contemplation on our life aims.

Before we come to the answer, we must grasp the force of the question. It has been often said that the human mind, if it probes deeply enough and honestly enough, will finally come upon the ultimate question, from which there is no escape and to which there is no final answer: Why is there something rather than nothing? The mystery of existence, any existence, lies at the heart of all subsequent investigation. That there is, is the ultimate mystery.

It is this question, particularized to the human situation, that our prayer begins by asking. Why are any of us here? What is the basis of this brief bout of life nestled between two darknesses? The initial answer to these questions is not what we might expect from a book of prayer. "For the multitude of human deeds are hollow, and the days of mortal life vain before You; and the human being is not preeminent over the beast, for all is futile." Echoing Ecclesiastes, the prayer emphasizes that death (the "futility" in the preceding quotation) is the ultimate end of both beast and human. Here indeed, in capsule form, is the very situation described in chapter 3. Human achievement cannot escape the specter of death, which makes our existence, our grandiose designs and heights of accomplishment, equivalent to that of the beasts, for we, like they, will die.

The prayer book will not leave this despairing image as its last word, and indeed the answer to the dilemma is what we might anticipate. In the Hebrew, it takes only three words: *aval anachnu amcha,* "But we are Your people." The answer is in relationship. God, we presume to speak of our life as valuable and our works as precious because we are objects of concern to You. Because we are about to pray and enter into dialogue with You. We are important because we are about to make the offering of the heart that You ask of us, and to grant a request of God is no small thing.

Even a glance at this section of the preliminary prayers illustrates the recurrent motifs of prayer: relationship, worth, need.

A listening God is the critical figure in prayer. For prayer is a plea to be heard. We speak too often to an empty cosmos of wishes none can share, certain that our words spin out into the indifferent atmosphere, to dissipate and disappear along with all the vain, unheeded wishes of humanity. If only we would be heard!

That we are heard is the central conviction of prayer. Prayer does not rise or fall upon the granting of a wish. That is the prayer of a child who views heaven as a celestial dispensary of gifts. As often as not our requests are denied. In the epigraph to this chapter we note that the Psalmist loves to know that God *listens* to his prayer, not grants his prayer. But we are granted the object of prayer itself, and that is to be heard.

One of the most moving prayers of the High Holiday service has as its theme the simple plea *shma kolenu*—"hear our voice." The voice of the community rises as one. There are varieties in the individual wishes and hopes of those in the community, but one shared aspiration, cutting across all the divides of humanity, is to be heard, to be heeded.

True prayer is liberation. It releases the imaginings and yearnings of a soul, relieves—even if only for a moment—the fear of being alone, of never being understood. "Although the distance from earth to heaven is a journey of five hundred years, when one whispers a prayer, or even meditates in silence, God is nearby and hears" (Deut. R. 2:10).

Prayers can arise from specific occasions as well and express the spectrum of human emotion, from gratitude to wonder to dread. So the very sight of a mountain or a rainbow evokes a blessing and a remembrance of the rainbow's function in the Bible as the covenant with Noah. Again, the form of the blessing is significant and displays its true intent. "Blessed are You" begins each blessing, before switching into the more deferential third person. The mountain is impersonal in its grandeur; the rainbow shines equally for all who care to look. They are instantly personalized, however, because they become triggers for the intimacy of the individual's relationship with God. The mountain's striking beauty evokes blessing from us, and in that evocation is the connection prayer can forge in our lives. The tie between aesthetics and dialogue is made clear. God has fashioned an often beautiful world, and our enjoyment of it is one more reason to renew the intimacy of our connection with Him.

Prayer is a means not only of expressing emotion, but of shaping and defining it. With prayer we can sharpen our perceptions of human yearning. Certain common feelings require expression. They must be given a form so that we can speak them properly, for we cannot all invent our own language. To say "I love you" is a kind of liturgical formula: it allows a deep feeling to be expressed in a routine manner that is understood by those to whom we speak as well as allowing a release of our own feelings about the subject. Similarly, the formulae of prayer offer the opportunity to say that which might otherwise remain unsaid. How shall we express gratitude for simply being alive or feeling well (a rare enough gift) or having enough to eat? We often feel such appreciation, but it is buried for lack of avenues of expression. To what or whom shall we speak when the fullness of well-being moves us, inspires gratitude?

A wise Rabbinic maxim predicts that at the end of days all the sacrifices will be abolished save the Thanksgiving offering (Lev. R. 9:7). In an ideal world, when pain has been erased, people will still need to express their thanks, and one avenue that has been profitably walked by generations is that of prayer.

A frequently asked question is why God needs prayer. To this, the tradition offers two distinct answers. The first is quite simply that God needs prayer to the extent that He needs (or, better, wishes) to have communication with His creations. Judaism presupposes that God cares for and wishes to relate to human beings. For that reason alone prayer is important.

The second answer is that God does not truly "need"

prayer, human beings do. It makes no difference to God's "self-conception" that I praise or glorify Him. The difference to my self-conception, on the other hand, is profound. I am reminded of my station and task in this world. For a moment it strikes me anew that my life is a gift, tenuous, fleeting, and that I owe the granting of that gift to God. Exalting God brings home to me my limitations, often hard to recall in a world where human endeavor has done so much, achieved so stupendously.

This explains the Rabbinic regulation concerning bowing during the Amidah, the central prayer of the Jewish worship service. A regular worshiper bows at the beginning and end of two of the benedictions. A high priest bows at the beginning of each of the eighteen blessings, and a king remains bowed for the entire prayer (Ber. 34 a, b). The greater the temptation to pride, the more one must be humbled. The greater the position we attain in this world, the more we need to recall that each of us is human, each of us needs guidance and mercy.

Like all human behavior, the ability to express gratitude can be squelched by disuse. Taking this world, and ourselves, for granted is one of the great and seductive errors of humanity. There is no trick to being grateful for that which is rare and special. To be grateful for that which is always there is difficult. Prayer helps us to appreciate that thanks are due for blessings that accompany us throughout life, blessings that are indispensable but often overlooked.

Prayer is the sustained language of the spirit, ever deepening, reaching to express the deepest centers of the soul. The *bracha*, the blessing, is the spiritual epigram in which the essence of the individual's relationship to God is pithily and memorably put. Both are parts of the larger web of the Jewish relationship to God, one often misunderstood. To understand the Jewish God, one must first come to grips with Jewish learning and Jewish practice.

STUDY

The scholar Dr. Louis Finkelstein once remarked, "When I pray, I speak to God. When I study, God speaks to me." Study enables one to hear the voice of God as mediated by history and tradition. In the Torah, Talmud, the libraries of commentaries, discussion, and discourse, Jews have found voices whose separate tones join in a larger symphonic meditation on the meaning of life and the providence of God.

Reading and study have always been a cornerstone of Jewish life, the intellectual anchor to the emotive experiences of prayer and wonder at the world. In a famous phrase, Wordsworth defined poetry as "emotion recollected in tranquillity." Study embodies the reflected-upon passion of religious experience, the sages' attempt to crystallize what has been gleaned from the direct encounter with life and loss. A religious text is the distillation of dialogue between human beings and God.

Many of these texts are ancient, and we live in a world that venerates the newborn. Much *is* new in this world, and there is a great deal about which the Rabbis could not have dreamed. The universe we inhabit has been transformed by technology. We speak a different language. Our clothes, communications, and social network are not what the second-century Babylonian knew, or what his forebear in the deserts of Sinai could have possibly imagined. And yet we study their words. Why?

Putting aside questions about the Divine or human nature of the text, study of the Bible or the Talmud presupposes something that grants an insight into all religious tradition. It recognizes first that nearly everything about our human situation is new. We speak different languages from those of our predecessors, have different cultural and political structures, live in new lands and under new circumstances. Technology has revolutionized the world. Everything is new—save the nature of human beings. There are no new kinds of tears: we cry the same tears as did David for his child. The same sibling rivalries plague households today that disturbed the domestic peace of Abraham and Sarah, of Jacob and Leah. People feel pain, joy, and hope as they did five hundred and three thousand years ago. The sacred texts of Judaism speak to human beings, and human beings have not changed; they can learn from the struggles of others to find their way through life. What the Greeks said of Plato is equally true of the Rabbis and sages of religious tradition—wherever we go in life, we meet them on the way back.

We strive to know the same God. The long tradition of Jewish texts is a chronicle of the attempt to understand ourselves and our Creator. Nothing about that has changed. The pages of the search have yellowed, the bindings cracked, but the words retain their fire and force. Ancient books are not scoured simply to confirm the insights of modern psychology; such a pursuit is an error as foolish as it is pervasive. All too often we are delighted with the wisdom of a tradition that somewhere endorses the same view trumpeted in today's feature magazine piece. But tradition is there to teach what we *do not know,* or what we have forgotten. Not all the apparatus of modern science, despite its stupendous array, will tell us what to live for or why we are here. No psychologist—clinical, behavioral, cognitive, or Freudian—can pronounce to us what it is to be good, how to become holy.

An intriguing Midrash explains the Jewish understanding of the value and the limitation of books:

When Moses and Aaron came to Pharaoh to plead in God's name for freedom, Pharaoh asked, "Who is this God of whom you speak? I have never heard His name! But wait, I shall search through all the records in my library, perhaps in the archives there is some mention of Him." When he found only the names of pagan gods, and no reference to the God of Israel, Pharaoh dismissed Moses and Aaron with the words "He is not found in my books; there is no God such as the One in whose name you speak." (Ex. R. 5:14)

There is a double irony in this Midrash. First, it is foolishness on the part of Pharaoh, when surrounded by the enormous power and majesty of God, to assume that because God is not detailed in some ancient tome, He cannot exist. This is the folly of those who assume that, as God has not been measured and recorded, because God cannot be found in the respected journals of science and medicine, He must be a delusion. If He cannot be demonstrated by the vast apparatus of modern learning, He must not exist! No matter our ignorance in other areas. The hubris of modern empiricism here is astonishing—if we cannot see God in our instrumentation, He is suspect. In this we are certain: God is not in the books and so cannot be. The Midrash views this attitude with wry and saddened amusement.

The second irony of the Midrash is that Judaism believes that God *can* be found in books, if one searches in the right books. This is the essence of study, to hear the mediated voice of God. "The study of God's word is greater than the rebuilding of the Temple" (Meg. 16b). For although the Temple was once the premier means of relating to God, study has opened that gate at any time, in any place. It is the Rabbinic conviction that the study of text can lead one to a knowledge of and a relationship with the Lord.

Here is the ambivalence of all learning. Life is not found in books, to be sure, but there *is* life in books. Sacred texts make the world come alive; they change perspective, shape vision. They are the whetstones upon which the intellects and imaginations of the ages have been sharpened. Learning, knowing, is an essentially religious activity in the Jewish scale of value. One reason for this is quite simple. God created the world, and to know of His creation in its beauty and intricacy is a religious task. Moreover, the human mind was provided in order that we use it, and the intelligent use of the tools we were given is also a task of spirit.

Deeper still is the fervent excitement of learning known to those who have taken a difficult problem, grappled with it, and finally grasped it. To know the joy of intellectual challenge is to feel that its roots go deeper than simple problem solving. The great eighteenth-century scholar Elijah of Wilna was quoted as saying that he preferred a lifetime of searching to an assurance of answers. There is a certain sense of peace and harmony that reigns with the conquest of difficult intellectual terrain. This is not elitism, for the joy occurs on all levels of study and struggle. The simplest problem yields the same type of joy as the profoundest difficulty. The deep delight of learning, which is a sort of religious rapture, occupies a central place in the ritual life of Judaism.

So long as Jewish books and Jewish learning exist, Judaism will survive. Today that learning is both easier and more difficult to attain than ever. Most of us face a difficult barrier of language. The languages of sacred texts, Hebrew and Aramaic, have become strange to us. Yet there are also more books of Jewish learning being published in English right now than in any language at any time in history. In a very traditional Jewish sense, God has never been more accessible than now. No field of Jewish study lies untended: Bible, history, philosophy, Talmud, prayer, theology, how-to: the list is never-ending. All the books are there, waiting only to be questioned, argued with, listened to. The aim throughout the ages is the same: for each generation to be both anthologist and author; to preserve what was, and to create anew.

RITUAL/MITZVOT
BETWEEN HUMAN BEINGS AND GOD

Ritual is language. The exploding study of symbols (semiotics) makes it increasingly clear that the network of symbols and rituals that tie a faith system together shares many characteristics with language. Like language, ritual imparts specific messages, it grows and changes, speaks more fully to those conversant with the system, telling of things that are not directly spoken, but are suggested, hinted at, understood by "fluent speakers."

Think of a candle lit for the Sabbath. What a complex and varied tale is told by that simple light! First, lighting is the fulfillment of a ritual obligation. The glow portends the coming of the Sabbath. Simultaneously, memories are evoked by other homes the world over, throughout history, illuminated by that same modest light on a Friday night. The sanctity of the day is signaled in its flame, in the way the Sabbath is divided from the week as light is divided from darkness. In the glow is a glimmer of the original creation that the Sabbath commemorates.

All of this and a great deal more is implicit in the lighting of a candle for the Sabbath. It is an immemorial sign for the Jewish people. Above the ark in every synagogue there hangs a lamp called "the eternal light" that is to remain lit. But of course, when the synagogue, or the city, or the civilization ends, when it is no more, the light will be extinguished. There is no eternal light—save the Sabbath candles. They have been lit over the span of centuries, in different cultures and lands, never extinguished, ever renewed. As one looks at such a rich symbol from various sides, the language becomes both clearer and more expressive, progressively deeper.

One more level brings us again to our familiar destination: the Sabbath candle too is a reflection of the dialogue

between human beings and God. The first two manifestations of this are evident: First is the blessing, prescribed
upon the lighting of Sabbath candles on Friday night,
"Blessed are You, O God, King of the universe, who has
sanctified us with Your commandments, and ordained the
lighting of the Sabbath candles." The action is tied directly
to the will of God. Second, the entire experience of the
Sabbath, the day of rest, is in emulation of God's conduct of
resting after creation—one more form of the *Imitatio Dei* we
spoke about in chapter 4.

But a somewhat subtler point is suggested by the word-
ing of the blessing: "who has sanctified us." The Sabbath
candle represents the raising of life to a plane of sanctity.
Sanctity is the domain of God; one who enters a realm of
sanctity enters the realm in which the Divine and human
meet. Here one enters into dialogue with God.

Ritual is the magic looking glass of access to that other
world. Sometimes, like the subtle flourish of a great actor,
it is the apparently negligible gesture that holds volumes of
meaning. As the *t'fillin*, the phylacteries whose donning
accompanies the morning prayer service, are wrapped about
one's finger, the verse from Hosea is recited: "And I will
betroth you to Me forever, yea, I will betroth you to Me in
righteousness and in justice, in loyalty and in love. And I
will betroth you to Me in faithfulness, and you shall know
the Lord." Could there be a more direct illustration of relation blooming in ritual? A wound strap of leather is suddenly transformed into the metaphorical engagement ring
between a human being and God. Ritual has provided the
opening through which meeting can take place.

A ritual act becomes poignant when done with a consciousness of its meaning. There is drama, even daring, in
this human confrontation with God. Every ritual act is a
risk: it risks emptiness if the performer is unaware or un-
willing to feel its enormity, and it risks—as does prayer—

the feeling of having offered without return. The paradox of religious action lies here: fullness of response is felt only when the individual has performed the action with trust that response will be forthcoming. In another context, the Talmud remarks that "halves are not granted in heaven" (Yoma 69b). In ritual, halves are not granted here on earth. That which is easily done will not sweep the worshiper into a sense of communion or communication with God. In the Bible, when God spurned Cain's offering to Him, it was not because Cain offered nothing. The text tells us that Cain offered "from the fruit of the soil" (Gen. 4:3). He was rejected because he refused to offer of his best.

How to offer one's best, and what that means, is difficult to pin down. Whether a mitzvah, a commandment, requires *kavvanah* (a combination of enthusiasm, intent, and intensity) is a continuing debate in the Talmud. Many believe that one's obligation is fulfilled if the action is performed, regardless of the fervor or lack of fervor with which it is done. But in the attempt to establish a relationship with God, empty action, however appropriate, does not suffice. Like all relationships that aim at depth, opening up to God, whether in ritual or prayer, demands passion. God is found by searching with one's entire being, not in the mechanical repetition of rite, however hallowed. There must be a combination of ritual, prayer, purpose.

RITUAL/MITZVOT
BETWEEN ONE PERSON AND ANOTHER

Human beings are created in the image of God. This central assertion from the book of Genesis points our way to the second category of mitzvot. For God is spoken to and served in our interactions with human beings. Our dealings with other people are not separable from reverence for the Divine.

To be good is also to be devout. To help another is to worship God. Or as the Midrash puts it, "When one person greets another it is as if he greets the Divine presence" (Mechilta, Amalek).

A painful constant of human life is that intimacy often breeds a callous indifference. People are frequently more deferential to strangers, acquaintances at work, those whom they barely know and do not care for, than they are to family and friends. *Tadir ush'ayno tadir, tadir kodem,* a venerable principle in Jewish law, says that the frequently performed mitzvah or precept takes precedence. Too often this law is violated in interpersonal life, when the infrequent, the novel, takes precedence, and close relationships take a backseat. On those dearest to us we sometimes expend the least effort to be kind, patient, forgiving. Yet relationship with God is prepared for by our relationships with human beings, and if we cannot love close, how will we love Ultimacy? "The one who loves his fellow creatures will be loved by God" (Shab. 151b).

Ethics begin with those close to us, but they cannot end there. The network of relationships is as wide as this world and ties us together with each other and with God. Ethical precepts and moral conduct are every bit as much a part of relation to God as is prayer. In Judaism it is not a function of kindly largess to give charity. It is a mitzvah, a commandment, and with it, one not only betters the lot of another person, but honors God.

This is the simplified essence of Martin Buber's conception of relationship. At certain times, if we are receptive and sensitive enough, we truly encounter other people, see them in the fullness of their humanity, view them not as means by which some need or other of our own in this world can be met, but as ends in themselves. Through this sort of deep encounter with another person we glimpse the ultimate encounter, the encounter with God. This general approach, variously expressed, is a natural result of what we have learned up to this point. Human beings are to emulate God, for we are created in His image. Therefore it is to be expected that one's treatment of others will be a direct reflection of one's relationship to God. We touch eternity in our own temporality, in our treatment of this time-saturated world in which we move and live.

Now the theory behind the Rabbinic portrayal of God's human characteristics becomes a bit clearer. Why does God visit Abraham on his sickbed and console Jacob in his mourning (Gen. R. 8:13)? Because such action illustrates, more dramatically than any exhortation, just what it means to be "godly" and to honor God. "What is our life?" asks the prayer, and the tradition answers, It is the sum of your desires and deeds, which translated means the sum of your relationship to God, partially reflected in your treatment of other people.

In Exodus 33:13, when Moses wants to come to know God, he asks Him: "Show me *Your ways* that I may know You" (emphasis added). When God wishes to know human beings, they are subject to the same question. We are known by our ways. We come to know God not only through meditation on the marvels of this world, through the direct dialogue of prayer and the ultimate language of ritual, but through our ways, through our paths in this life, through the ethical standards that we uphold or ignore.

Goodness is the most difficult task enjoined upon human beings. Dramatic single gestures grab attention and acquire the luster of heroism; but it is the daily, draining effort to be kind, to rise above pettiness, irritation, and limitation, that is truly arduous, and praiseworthy. In his famous summary statement of human purpose, the prophet Micah declares: "He has told you, O man, what is good, and what the Lord requires of you: Only to do justice, to love mercy, and to walk humbly with your God" (Micah 6:8). This may well be the most understated "only" on record. The task is immense and unrelenting. But to the prophet, the simplicity is not in the task, *but in the choice.* This is what each person simply must strive for, and concerning that injunction Micah assumes there can be no question.

Without God, values are a human creation, and so subject to uprooting by human beings. If our conception of morality derives only from our own thought, then morality is reduced to a matter of opinion, and its variation from society to society is not a result of some having progressed more than others, but merely of each viewing what is right and wrong differently. So we cannot truly condemn others, no matter how repugnant their actions seem to us. Only a supreme power can offer objective ethics to the world. In the very existence and presence of God, in the possibility of human encounter with Him, morality finds the plank upon which it is built. The prophetic message is ripe with meaning: humanity cannot by itself create the structures and institutions by which to live. Our intelligence outruns our wisdom, a frightening phenomenon, and we need to have certain standards that cannot be undermined by the dialectical ingenuity or moral lassitude that often characterizes human life. Such standards can only be Divine. In reaching up toward God, one becomes conscious of earthly demands as well, those so succinctly summarized in the prophet's words that we pursue justice, love mercy, and walk humbly with God.

Divinity as the centerpiece of moral behavior is emphasized in Rabbi Akiba's statement that when one deceives another he trespasses against "the Third One" (Sifra on Lev. 5:21). Behind all human conduct is the third participant, effected by the social arrangements and actions of human beings. A supreme moral principle of Judaism is that one never acts in the human realm alone. A sin against another human being is a sin against God, and both must be asked forgiveness. The "Third One" is part of the moral drama of our lives as well.

CONCLUSION

It may seem strange to conclude a discussion of ritual with a panegyric to moral behavior. Traditionally, however, the two were intertwined; there was no clear distinction between ritual and moral behavior. There is an ethical component to ritual behavior that is taken very seriously by Judaism. Having explored the centrality of God, we can understand the ethical content of ritual. Ritual awakens and sustains one's relationship to God, which is itself the ground of all morality.

Nonetheless, morality is not the essence of Judaism, as some interpreters argue. Crucial as it is, there is evidence aplenty in the Jewish tradition that if a single critical factor can be isolated, it is the individual's and the people's relationship to God. Morality is a prime factor in that relationship, but not the only one.

The greatest figure in Jewish history is Moses. We have seen in the Midrash quoted in chapter 3 how the Rabbis venerated this remarkable individual. Maimonides, the premier Jewish thinker of the Middle Ages, articulated as a fundamental principle of Judaism that no prophet had ever arisen in Israel as great as Moses. Moses is clearly, unequivocally, the paradigm of a Jewish religious figure.

In the Bible, at the end of his life, how is Moses praised? Is he called the most moral individual on earth? Does the Bible say that Moses observed the highest percentage of mitzvot? No. Although it is taken for granted that Moses is a moral giant, that he followed God's word with all his might, that is not his epitaph. Rather, his praise is that he experienced God "face to face" (Deut. 34:10). Moses had the most comprehensive and intimate relationship with God. We grant the relationship would have been impossible had Moses not been a moral hero, but it is relationship that is the ultimate praise, the desired end.

Covenant—in Hebrew, *brit*—is the central illustration of this religious truth. The idea of covenant lies at the heart of Jewish life. It is a contract, a relation between human beings and God. Again, a pivotal part of that contract is the agreement to be good. However, goodness is only a slice of the overall agreement, which also includes rituals and attitudes with no necessary moral consequence. We might define the Jewish position as the search for ethics in the context of Divine-human dialogue.

The "language" detailed above is the Jewish system of human relations with God, however briefly and inadequately represented by this single chapter. God Himself participates in the system enjoined upon human beings, a "poetic conceit" that emphasizes the importance of spiritual language. In the Rabbinic depictions, God studies Torah and even wears t'fillin and prays (Ber. 7a)! In other words, all that human beings are enjoined to do to communicate with God, He is envisioned as doing on His own as well. No clearer image could be conjured of the reciprocal nature of relationship. God communes with Himself and with humanity, and our sense of that communion is not far removed from our own dialogue with God.

We have been educated to understand that communication between human beings takes place on multiple levels: in speech, in the motions of our bodies, in a glance. Much time and attention has been devoted lately to the examination of "nonverbal communication." This was a lesson Judaism recognized long ago. The motions of prayer say something that cannot be said with words alone. Wrapping t'fillin around one's finger while reciting the beautiful betrothal verse from Hosea is a symbol that cannot be duplicated in any other medium. Bowing during prayer is an acknowledgment of humility more affecting than any self-effacing speech. Beating one's breast makes regret resound inside, evoking a feeling of sorrow at one's lapses in life that is deeper than any verbal formula. Ritual is the total language.

Part of entry into Judaism, as with any culture, religion, or civilization, is learning the language. A tragedy of modern Jewish life is that this language is foreign to so many Jews, so many who might be native speakers. It can be learned, however, with some time, some study and diligence. Like any system, Judaism unfolds its riches gradually, and increased application yields increased rewards. As the sage says of the Torah in the Rabbinic work Pirke Avoth: "Turn it over and over, for everything is in it" (5:24).

Ideally this partnership of dialogue would always be possible. Yet we find with God as with other human beings that there is a sense, all too often, of being cut off, unable to join in any kind of communication or dialogue. With all the resources of language, verbal and ritual, a break appears between the individual soul and others. In trying to link ourselves up we sometimes encounter only distance, and we learn anew a lesson of Jewish history taught first at the beginning of the Bible. We are all, each of us, in exile, and part of the human mission is the desperate search to find a way home.

7

The Two Exiles

"You are strangers and residents with me."
—Leviticus 25:23

How can one be both a stranger and a resident? The text
may be explained as follows: God is saying—If you feel too
comfortable in this world, too much like residents, I will
be a stranger to you. But if you do not feel entirely at home
in this world, if you feel a bit like strangers yourselves, I
will be a resident—I will dwell among you.
—The Maggid of Dubnov, *Ohel Ya'acov*

The mythic history of humanity begins in exile. After vi-
olating God's admonition not to eat from the tree of knowledge, Adam and Eve are cast out from Eden. This often
invoked myth has been interpreted from various viewpoints:
as a story about human sinfulness, about the beginnings of
sexuality, childbearing pain, toil on the land, and so forth.
Still, the heart of the story is about what it means to humanity to be forced from paradise.

The expulsion from the garden tells a metaphysical not a
geographic truth. Human beings are essentially estranged,
plucked from the original paradise, doomed to an exile as
long as history itself. Here begins the irreparable break:
paradise is lost and we are forever far from home.

Exile as the primal punishment is emphasized in the
drama that follows expulsion from the garden, the murder
of Abel. Cain is fated by God to be a wanderer on the earth.

The greatest of sins, murder, finds its punishment in the perpetual human predicament, exile. Cain will have no home, he will be a "ceaseless wanderer" on the earth. Having been the first to decisively reject the humanity of another, his brother, he will be the first refugee. The text itself is unequivocal about the severity of Cain's punishment. Lest the reader think that being a wanderer is not fit retribution for so heinous a crime, Cain's anguish makes the reverse quite clear: "And Cain said to God, 'My punishment is too great to bear!' " (Gen. 4:13). Homelessness is for Cain the cruelest fate.

His punishment is ours as well. Exile will not leave us alone. In this generation, its ravages are imprinted on our souls: pictures of people fleeing in boats, marching from their towns and villages and countries, clambering to escape when home is made hellish by the demonic touch of other human beings. Ours is the age of "boat people," an entire generation of people forced from home, propelled out to sea on rafts and flimsy fishing crafts, heading toward unknown destinations, their dwellings transferred from the land of their ancestors to splintered, swaying planks of wood. The human tale is written here in tragic strokes, the embodiment of an eternal predicament: being without a true home.

The pain of exile reaches into contemporary art and literature. Prominent in the authorial chorus of our troubled age is the bittersweet sound of expatriate voices. In a new language, in a different land and culture, artists try to regain their bearings, writing of home ever more eloquently for its loss. Homelessness in all its forms is a motif of our time.

Cries of exile have echoes deep in the Jewish tradition. Sobs and pleas of the exiled are heard in the Bible, the Talmud, the medieval literature, echoes of an ancient agony that still persists. Exile is shared in different ways by each of us. When the Psalmist, in the classic condensation of exilic despair, asks, "How can we sing in a strange land"

(Ps. 137:4), we instantly understand the question: Can happiness be found in a new, alien, and difficult culture? More fundamentally, even without physical displacement, can anyone feel at home in this world no matter where he is, no matter how agreeable the surroundings?

Exile laces the fabric of history and modernity, but it is of different kinds. Still, there are two sides of human exile that touch every life, touch even those fortunate enough to be geographically at home: the exile from the world, and the exile from the self.

To feel exiled in the world is not a matter of geographic dislocation, although exile from one's physical homeland is a political and historical symbol of it. Just as one exiled from a homeland can never feel fully comfortable elsewhere, never have a territory in which he or she feels at home, the concept of exile from the world suggests that we can never be fully comfortable in this world. The image of the physically exiled touches us in part because he or she is inside us no matter the course of our own lives, and we intuitively identify with the fear and wrenching sense of being dispossessed.

Exile from self has been portrayed in many ways in our time, most often with the catchall term "alienation." Like "world exile," this "exiled self" is seemingly an inescapable part of being human. Both are true and deep. They are in some ways distinct, but looking at each in turn, we will discover the single arena where they join, the summation of the idea of exile, estrangement, loss.

EXILE FROM THE WORLD

How can one be exiled from this world, the locus of life, which we are fated to call home? This world is the only arena we know. If we are separated from it, perhaps that is the inevitable lot of mankind. For if we cannot be at one with the environment in which we pass all our natural lives, in which we grow and raise children, laugh and love and die, then does unity or oneness have any true meaning? To speak of unity with the world might be to hope for something that can never be.

That commonsense answer begins to shift and slip when we look closer into our own souls. Some of the apparently natural estrangement is in fact attributable to the nature of our society. In order to survive in this world we need to insulate ourselves from it. The Swiss writer Max Frisch declared technology to be "the knack of so arranging the world that we need not experience it." We live in fortresses, formidable buildings that regulate the weather, control the cycles of nature, enable us to work in a drenching rain as we would on a sun-soaked day. The most elementary connections with the earth, with growth, are something to be sought or carefully cultivated, to be experienced on an idle vacation or a determined mission, as opposed to the natural daily occurrence that was the rule in earlier times. Crops are packaged and presented, plants bought at a nursery. Animals are esoteric and to be viewed at the zoo. Instantly upon entering our society we begin the resolute dislocation from the world we are pleased to call home.

With reservations, this is a price we willingly pay. To be subject to the elements is to be unable to fend off frost, storms; nature is not always as kind as her staunch and forgetful advocates sometimes suppose. Still, our relationship to nature has changed profoundly in the modern world. Abandoning our partnership, we have become the manipulators of nature, sometimes with tragic results. Our inability to feel nature in our bones, to see ourselves as part of it in the way that earlier societies took for granted, has resulted in insensitivity and near catastrophe.

Perhaps the easiest way to understand the depth of this dislocation is to recognize the astonishing return of a prophetic concept we have long disregarded. As happens so often, an ancient message has taken on a renewed urgency.

The biblical prophets preached that if human beings misbehaved or were morally lacking, the world itself would rebel against them. The mountains would shudder, the earth dry up, the entire natural order take vengeance for the moral turpitude of human beings. One of the most eloquent statements of this kind comes from the prophet Amos:

> Listen to this, you who devour the needy, annihilating the poor of the land, saying ". . . We will buy the poor for silver, the needy for a pair of sandals. . . ." Shall not the earth tremble for this, and all who dwell on it mourn? . . . "And in that day," declares my Lord God, "I will make the sun set at noon, I will darken the earth on a sunny day. I will turn your festivals into mourning, and all your songs into dirges." (Amos 8:4–10)

As humanity progressed, we realized that cause and effect were hardly so neat. A despicable human being, a depraved nation, would not cause an earthquake or a tornado. The advent of science destroyed belief in the nexus between morality and natural events. In Bertrand Russell's succinct phrase: "People used to say that faith moved mountains, and no one believed it. Now we say that the atom bomb moves mountains, and everyone believes it."

But Russell's words hint at the renewal of the prophetic message, albeit in a new way. For we have learned that if we do not have some moral concern for our world, the natural order will indeed rebel against us. If we do not take care to limit the pollutants pouring into our atmosphere, the air will be poison and the protective layer above our world destroyed. If we explode the weapons we have fashioned, the world will, much in the manner of Amos's apocalyptic depiction, become darkness at midday, and turn all our feasts into mourning. Once again the idea of linkage between moral behavior and the natural order is current and frightening.

Surely part of this problem is our increasing unfamiliarity with the feeling that we are a part of the natural world. The Bible grants human beings stewardship of the earth, but nowhere suggests that we are apart from the chain of being on this planet. With the advent of science, and our increasing ability to arrange the world to suit our needs, it has become harder and harder to remind ourselves of the elementary truth that we are bound up in the fate of our world irrevocably, inescapably. Our sense of exile from the natural order is not only painful, it is terribly dangerous.

In the biblical story of Noah, the promise God makes to humanity is that He will not destroy the world again. For millennia that promise was a comfort. But for our time it contains a chilling omission: God does not promise to prevent us from destroying ourselves.

Still, technology is only a reflection of a deeper dislocation, not the ultimate cause of human estrangement from the natural order. Exile transcends any given society, and we should not think ourselves condemned by the wonders of modernity to wander alone among the generations, unconnected to the globe that bore us.

The essence of human exile is the break between ourselves and the natural order. I can see the clouds, count the stars, feel the world through all my human senses, but it is *out there,* separate from me, and I cannot enter into it, or it into me. There are boundaries beyond which we can never move, the boundaries set by our physical being, our bodies. The flip side of individuality—the joy of being a person distinct from all others and all else—is that I cannot fully join in the world. Exile is a pushing away, a disunion, and in this we are exiled from earth. We can dwell on it, but we cannot merge with it because we are separate sentient creatures with our own distinct consciousness, creatures cased inside our own finite shells.

This same sense of exile from the world is true of our relationships with other people. We do not usually think of ourselves as "exiled" from others, but we are, and in much the same way as from the world around us, although here the problems of estrangement are aggravated.

We are all irrevocably cut off from the thoughts of others. Of the myriad thoughts and impressions that pass through our minds each day, only a small fraction can be shared. Thought is a process that goes on inside, and no one else has access to the inner workings of our minds. Indeed, we do not always have access ourselves. Even with those to whom we are close, whom we love, we cannot in the end share the fullness of our ideas, imaginations, desires— expression is not adequate nor time sufficient. How many thoughts are left unexpressed in the passage of a single day! Much of what we think is a slight fragment, too ethereal for the substantiality of words, too brief to be captured. A degree of exile from others is the inevitable product of the failings of language. Sometimes we think language closes the gap, but it only reinforces its existence. A friend or relative suddenly says something unexpected. There is joy in that, to be sure—she or he still retains the capacity to surprise. But there is also pain, the pain of realizing that however intimate, for however long a time, two people will always be partly strangers to each other, that each will always have thoughts the other cannot share, would not fathom. There is an interpersonal exile that afflicts each of us. There is no complete union of souls.

The original connotation of the word *individual* is wholeness, that which cannot be divided. But it means, just as surely, that which cannot be fully joined. We can be more or less at home, create structures that embrace or estrange.

Still, one must remain always outside other people, other worlds. Finally, to be "individual" is to acknowledge that exile is the eternal state of the human being.

EXILE FROM THE SELF

Separation from others is not the final stage of the human exilic experience. Ultimately, the most frightening exile is from oneself. "To be estranged from one's self" is a phrase that has grown less and less foreign in the past few centuries. We are accustomed, in our psychological and therapeutic age, to the idea that we are only dimly aware of what goes on inside us. Forces that are literally the stuff of nightmares roil in the most placid minds. Stock notions are added to the common store in every age—ideas once revolutionary that are then taken for granted. Our age numbers among its contributions the certainty that none of us can fully know ourselves for we are the products and bearers of impulses that lie, glacierlike, far beneath the surfaces of daily conduct.

Losing a sense of centrality and control was a gradual process in human history. First we were told by advances of astronomy that the earth was not the center of the universe. We then discovered that we were descended from the animals with whom we supposed no real commonality. Finally, in our day, psychology teaches us that we do not even know what goes on inside our own heads. The dethronement of humanity has been completed. We do not even understand or control ourselves.

That we are strangers to our selves is a commonplace. But we are also strangers to our own souls. If there is an exile particularly characteristic of our time, it is spiritual. Evidence abounds, and nowhere more convincingly than in the very attempts of people in our own day to vigorously assert their spirituality. The search for one's true spirit in a past life is a tacit (if naive) admission of the insufficiency of spirit as it now stands. Seeking out ersatz gurus, marching off to retreats where people purport to speak with the voice of ancient seers, is not the ludicrous spectacle of indulgent self-seeking. It reflects, rather, the inability of the modern spirit to comprehend itself, to tap its resources and expand its abilities in the context of tradition and community.

Not surprisingly, because this search is disconnected from communal and historical roots, it turns into a glorification of the seeker, rather than a true spiritual search. The celebration of self is not the same as reaching for God. And it is, paradoxically, in reaching *beyond the self* that self-realization truly occurs. There is no surer sign of the impoverishment of the individual than one who is devoted entirely to the cultivation of individuality. As the Chasidic Preacher of Zlotzov commented, when Moses declares in Deuteronomy (5:5) "I stand between God and you," he teaches us that when a person thinks only of himself, and his own importance, then the "I" can stand between him and God.

Yet even those who seek in a tradition often find that the tradition which soothed and guided their ancestors seems alien, having been no part of their own upbringing. The vaunted search for roots is a spiritual search, a desire to have a place, to mitigate the inevitability of estrangement. Those who wish to find anew a tradition are acknowledging a painful truth of our time, that spirit has lost its moorings, and we are in exile from ourselves.

However frightening this image may be, there are glimmers of optimism in the word *exile* itself. Exile, or in Hebrew, *galut*, implies the possibility of returning home. Galut has no true meaning if it can never be reversed. While homecoming in an ultimate sense is the capstone of history, and cannot exist before the culmination of the drama, there is a remedy. As mentioned above, it consists in reaching beyond ourselves, in trying to link up with transcendence, to connect with that which ties all of creation together. There is one thing, one being, whose knowledge embraces all—humanity, nature, the self—and so negates the necessity of exile. That being is God.

EXILE AND TRANSCENDENCE

We have lost serious transcendence. For some, there is no transcendence. They live in this world with no thought of anything greater and are so weighted down by the anvils of the everyday that they cannot raise themselves above eye level. What cannot be seen does not exist. Exile is inevitable for those to whom we and our fellow creatures on earth are all that exists. For then this world was not designed for us, it is purposeless, and we walk upon it like unwelcome, powerful, and self-destructive invaders whose sojourn here is an accident of ancient chemistry. In some ways this scenario is worse than exile, for it denies the very possibility of a home. We are unaccountably here, in this temporary and unforgiving dwelling, with little more to do than huddle together awaiting the inevitable doom.

Others debase the notion of transcendence to support an unreasoned fanaticism or an ephemeral silliness. Among the former are nations or leaders who would ally the cause of the Creator with the agenda of the moment. God becomes the omnipotent ally of this or that social, cultural, or political cause. Among the latter are those who invoke God for anything from advertising strategies to cultist nonsense to football games. Again, "serious" transcendence is lost. The idea of transcendence serves as a political justification or a marketing tool. It is a term used for its effect, not for its meaning.

Before we can recover, we have to develop a sense of loss.

There is no homecoming until the pain of exile is sharp enough to disturb our nights and shadow our days. "Because of this our hearts are sick, because of these our eyes are dimmed" (Lamentations 5:17). So writes the author of a dirge on the exile from Israel. The keenness of the sense of loss is a combination of spiritual and physical dislocation. Though separated from us by more than two millennia, the anguished song of the exile still touches us and reminds us of our own, quite different, senses of exile.

The absence of spirit in life should be a constant gnawing pain at the center of our selves, never leaving us alone. The Bible makes clear that the danger of Egypt was not that slavery had decimated the Israelites, but that they had become comfortable in slavery. If that possibility existed in Pharaoh's Egypt, how much more possible is it in a society of comfort? Deprivation is a universal feeling—there is no human being who does not nurture hurt in his or her breast. To realize that we are depriving ourselves, that the spirit is being starved, and that it must be tended on a regimen of real effort and care is difficult. Serious transcendence is a transcendence that makes demands. One that acknowledges that above the human fray is that which not only makes us feel better, but at times makes us feel worse—for it imposes standards.

Our society fosters enormous concentration on externals: money, beauty, all the trappings of success that, however regularly derided and belittled, continue to dominate self-perception. (When you ask someone the revealing question "How much are you worth?" you are asking how much money he or she makes. Can there be any starker indicator of the outsized significance assigned to wealth than a phrase suggesting that human worth is ultimately monetary?)

What frequently goes unremarked, however, is that the much touted "new" concern for spirit is also largely a disguised concern for externals. Spiritual regimens promise increased performance at work and enhanced attractiveness to others. The enlightenment of the spirit has become another, albeit carefully marketed, technique for the satisfaction of the ego. It is not the exilic soul but the understuffed bank account that is on the line in such "journeys."

Expectation of what religion can and should do is the crux of the matter here. Distorted expectations have created an image of religion as one more hawker of the wares of satisfaction. A homecoming in a spiritual sense does not guarantee good looks or wealth. It aims at goodness and at communion with God. To be home is not to be rich. To be home is not to be "successful," however that word may be defined. To be home is not to be attractive. It is to seek meaning, to pursue goodness, to feel some sense of obligation. It is to be, in the final analysis, not alone.

THE EXILE OF GOD

Up to this point, we have spoken of "human" exile: from each other, the world, our selves. There is a higher, deeper level of exile as well.

"When Israel went into exile, the Divine presence went into exile along with them" (Pes. R. 31:5).

The fullness of exile is seen in the exile of God.

For all the daring of the Rabbis in speaking about God, no concept was more astonishing than this idea that God Himself was in exile. When the people were cast out of their land, the Midrash claims, God (or more precisely, the *Shechina*, the Divine presence) went with them, suffering the same pangs of exile. For the Rabbis, God is so in love with humanity that He will submit Himself to a kind of homelessness in the universe, a self-exile, to empathize with His beleaguered people.

There is a Kabbalistic notion, a concept of Jewish mysticism, that partakes of this spirit, the idea of *tsimtsum*. The mystics pose a problem of what we might call theological physics: If God is everywhere, if there is no inch of space not taken up by His presence, there is no room for the universe to be created. There must be space for "not-God" if separate creations, human beings and the physical world, are to be made. How then did God manage to create? He deliberately withdrew from part of the universe to make room for the world. The beginning of creation, its necessary onset, was the contraction of God into Himself. God is so devoted that He will perform that most difficult of acts: He will limit His scope, in order to create. In that self-constriction, say the mystics, begins creation, and thus God, too, with this cosmic self-effacement, has gone through a primal exile of which our exile is a reflection.

So appealing is the concept of God's exile, and so directly does it speak to the needs and fears of the Jewish tradition, that it has received startling expression in the Midrash: according to Rav Aha, God not only accompanied the people into exile, but God went, like his prophet Jeremiah, bound in chains! (Pes. de-R.K. 13:9)

Rav Aha's bold imagery expresses the idea that there is an element of self-constraint in God by which He exempts Himself from directing the historical process. God could have reversed the exile, of course, but chose to be bound like His creatures by the laws of the universe that He had established. It was not as He would have preferred—He was, after all, bound in those metaphorical chains—but as it must be. History is a reciprocal process; it is partly directed by God, but it is also the product of human beings, and so God is part captive of human action. That He is willing to so submit Himself, to share in all the experiences of hu-

manity including the most alienating and humiliating or-
deal of exile, is a startling affirmation of love and empathy,
of God's overriding concern for His creatures and creation.

God cannot enter fully into history, into our lives, if we
do not will it. Therefore the exile of God depends upon the
powers of human beings. This emphasizes our importance,
a point seized vigorously by the later mystics who made
much of this concept of the "exilic God." It empowers
human beings; it demonstrates our abilities to act in concert
with God to bring about redemption. When the burden is
shifted from God's action alone to a joint program, exile
becomes a call to human action, positing a scheme in which
the powers and responsibilities of human beings are fully
displayed. God does not redeem alone.

Is this to be taken literally, that God indeed exiled Himself? No, to assume an actual exile is beside the point, and
crosses the line from evocative imagery to theological arrogance. The symbolic sharing of fate between God and humanity is what is at stake. Why God exiles Himself in the
Jewish tradition is uncertain, but we know the framework
of God's character in the Jewish mind: compassionate, empathic, loving. So we imagine that God is exiled for the
reason that the Rabbis explain in the beautiful Midrash on
God's visit to Sodom. When the cities of Sodom and Gomorrah are to be destroyed, God says, "The outrage of Sodom
and Gomorrah is so great, and their sin so grave—I will go
down to see . . ." (Gen. 18:20–21). The Midrash, wondering why God "went down" to see rather than viewing the
horrendous spectacle from the heavenly heights, has a beautiful answer. "From this our sages taught that one should
not judge another until one comes into his place" (Midrash
Habiur). God went down so that He could be in the place
of Sodom, understand the sources of the people's actions,
perhaps ease His judgment.

Similarly, a God in exile permits us to feel that our

situation is shared and understood. The most characteristic human feelings of alienation and homelessness are not ours alone. In ways we cannot understand, manifestations that cannot be explained, God shares our pain, comprehends homelessness.

For however much it may seem limiting or "anthropomorphic" to speak of God understanding our feelings of displacement, it is surely more limiting to suggest God cannot understand. The greatest manifestation of God is not in the natural order—not in that display of power, artistry, and awe. For us, the greatest manifestation must be in the human heart, in the certainty, earned only after search and a sense of loss, that God comprehends, and feels with us.

THE EXILE FROM GOD

In some ways exile is the most inclusive of Midrashic concepts of God, for it suggests not only understanding, but also a commonality of experience. God endured the same horrible casting out as did the people. At first glance this appears to make Him subject to the currents of history: when earthly people are exiled, God goes with them.

There is another concept at stake, however, one that includes the exiles already elaborated above. God is not physically displaced, having dwelt once in Israel (as though He could be temporally located!) and now dwelling in a foreign land. Rather, God is separated from humanity, whether by sin or simple lack of care. This is the human exile of God. In this critical separation lies the greatest and deepest exile, and this is the summation of human exile from self and from the cosmos.

God comprehends both exilic forms because exile from the Creator is exile from the self, as well as exile from the Author of the universe, and so estrangement from the world.

We have now left geographical exile behind and are in the fullness of existential, spiritual loss.

In the Jewish tradition one cannot be truly home, no matter the geographical circumstances, if one is separate from God. Conversely, one cannot be fully exiled if with God. This magic of endurance granted Jews the ability to survive exile. Although there was a physical exile, the spiritual homecoming was ever imminent. The sense of being at home with God that suffused the prayers and daily life of the Jew, in whatever land at whatever age, was the true homecoming. I cannot call on God, feel that He is present, and still see myself as fully alien to the world around me.

Earlier in this chapter we quoted from Psalm 137, the classic psalm of exile, written in the wake of the expulsion to Babylonia. The Psalm reads in part:

> By the rivers of Babylon,
> there we sat,
> sat and wept,
> as we thought of Zion.
> There on the poplars
> we hung up our lyres,
> for our captors asked us there for songs,
> our tormentors, for amusement,
> "Sing us one of the songs of Zion."
> How can we sing a song of the Lord
> in a strange land?
> If I forget you, O Jerusalem,
> let my right hand wither;
> let my tongue stick to my palate
> if I cease to think of you,
> if I do not prize Jerusalem
> above all other joys.
>
> (Ps. 137:1–6)

After this wrenching lament, surely the people felt that however great God's care for them, that exile was unbearable. Yet part of the wonder and irony of this psalm is that, despite the genuine anguish, despite the vivid memory Jews retained of Israel throughout their exile, they did learn to do precisely that which the Psalm assumes is impossible—to sing a song of the Lord in a strange land. In exile, the Babylonian Talmud was written, the great academies of Babylonia were formed, a golden age of Jewish learning and creativity was celebrated. For so long as a people feels the presence of God, the pain of exile will not silence all song. Where God is, there home can be.

One of the most familiar epithets for God in the Talmudic tradition is *Makom*—meaning, simply, "place." *Makom* is understood to denote God's omnipresence. As Rabbi Ammi puts it, God is called Makom "because He is the place of His world" (Gen. R. 68:9), the world exists in His domain. In this simple term is the implication that God is the very reverse of exile, for exile is to be removed from Makom, from place. To dwell in God is to be home. Though this will not chase away the displacements of the world, its earthly exiles, real disappointments, and trials, it does allow a deeper feeling of rootedness in the universe. God is the ground of being, granting some sense of never truly leaving home.

If the pageant of life operates against such a backdrop, then to be placed in congruence with God is to fit, to feel the patterns mesh, to be partly pulled from the enveloping sense of alienation.

Today, God is not exiled with the people, but from the people. The difference is pivotal, decisive for the misdirection of our spiritual lives. When the children of Israel were forced from their land, the certainty of God's continual accompaniment eased the horror of the exile. Today, paradoxically, when most Jews do not feel the physical exile (even in many lands outside of Israel) and most modern arrangements are unprecedentedly kind to the Jewish people, the sense of estrangement from God is greater than at any time in our history.

The diagnosis is not simple, for far more is involved than a case of prosperity leading to unbelief. As we argue throughout this book, a whole range of factors combine to contribute to this unique estrangement. The worship of science (the *worship*, not the importance or prevalence of science that brings so many blessings) focuses us on tools and not their ultimate use; the blandness of much modern-day religion, with its emphasis on propriety and form rather than on the deeper issues of personal and communal destiny, which constitute the true core of any faith; the insensitivity to the true grandeur of humanity and the exaltation of our less admirable traits—all this and more creates a barrier to belief that is hard for the modern mind to vault.

We have in fact become estranged from the very idea of belief. So many ideals have exploded in our age that the act of belief itself seems to carry too many dangers. A sensitive soul today is tempted to swerve from commitments, since faiths of all sorts have proven false or even disastrous. Belief is often synonymous with credulity. History is a litany of earnest convictions that proved in the end to be folly. In each age people suffer because of the deeply held, and ultimately wrong, convictions of others. We do not wish to be added to the list of those caught in a darkening superstition in an enlightened age. When cloaked protectively by doubt, we will at least be spared the discomfort of feeling gullible.

Of course, avoiding all belief is an easy and ultimately unsatisfying answer. Yet we are just beginning to glimpse a stage beyond doubting, the stage when, as the pastor Harry Emerson Fosdick once remarked, we become mature enough to doubt our doubts.

Tying the exilic threads into one durable fabric, one

scheme we can understand and explore, combines all of these elements and more, placed against the background of distance from God. The haunting cry of exile from the Psalmist has become the lament of all. How can we sing in the modern age when our very accomplishments, as well as our brutality, render this world a strange land to us? How can we sing as strangers to ourselves?

That exile should become a central metaphor for us is no surprise. In some sense, life is a series of exilic experiences, remembered or not: from the womb, from the innocence of childhood, from home. The experience of Adam and Eve is eternal in human life, and everyone has the shattered rejection of paradise as part of the psychic scar of becoming a person.

The Bible sums this up in the initial command given by God to Abraham, the command that marks the beginning of the Jewish people. "Go forth," says God, "from your native land and from your birthplace and from the house of your father to the land that I will show you" (Gen. 12:1). Abraham must be wrenched from all that he knows to go to an unknown destination. That place will eventually be Israel, which in the Bible represents home. Yet even the trip home must begin in the call to exile.

Talk of exile and alienation is more than a parroting of the platitudes that have dominated much of the literature of the past forty years. Exile and alienation are summations of a time, one in which we have progressively learned that all is strange to us—the true composition of the world, the torturous twists of history, even what goes on inside our own minds. We have lost community with the universe. We have exiled ourselves.

Still, the weight of such a charge is more than we should be asked to bear alone. Many events have conspired to create this estrangement, and some were the price to be paid for a desirable progress. A denunciation of the modern world is often simply the last refuge of the inadequately adjusted. Unlike E. A. Robinson's Miniver Cheevy, who longs for prancing steeds and flashing swords, we cannot simply cough, call it fate, and keep on drinking. Escape is not a response, nor is mourning for some illusory, imagined perfect age gone by. We have to recognize what can be changed, and not pine for worlds that once were, for to live in memory alone destroys our chance for the only sane attitude in life, which is to live in hope.

Whether we can find the way home and stay safely on the path is *the* question of history, and of the personal life of each human being. Sometimes the greatest obstacles to safe arrival are not of our own making. If we feel strange in this world, is it not often a result of the catastrophes and horrors that are visited upon us? Exile is one way of saying that this earthly home has proved a very insecure place, less a refuge from the storms outside than a generator of them. Perhaps the responsibility for the exile must ultimately be placed not upon us but upon God. More than any technological estrangement, it is the continual tragedies of life that bid us feel unwanted, unwatched, unloved.

We must then turn finally to a question that haunts each confident, positive assertion in this book, that has doubtless troubled the reader again and again. One question has always been and will perhaps always be the bane of a believer and the greatest obstacle to one who would entertain belief. Each must continually wonder: If there is a good God, why is the world so often so awful? Why is there evil in God's world?

8

Evil in God's World

"If the Lord is with us, why has all this befallen us?"
—Judges 6:13

The discussion of a personal, compassionate God, a God who listens and cares, will inevitably strike some as jarring. Few ideas seem more out of touch with the pain and unfairness of this world. The foremost obstacle to religious belief, the presence of evil in a world governed by a benevolent God, haunts us as surely as it has every generation before us. Perhaps it is more horrible than in times past, for we live in the shadow of our own destruction, and still God is silent.

The taint of evil in human life varies, and the question of God's role presents itself in different forms throughout life. Although we are all aware of it as an abstract religious question, at moments of pain it becomes a personal affront, the question not only of the ages, but of the moment. Asking why evil exists in this world is often a veiled guise for asking why did *this* evil occur to *me*. Perhaps no other issue is at the same time so embracing and abstract and so individual, so concrete.

Believers of all descriptions and faiths have wrestled with the question of evil for as far back as we can see into recorded history—and doubtless long before doubts found the immortality of parchment and scroll. Contrary to what many may think, it is not true that to the nonbeliever there are no answers, and to the believer there are no questions. To the believer there are questions aplenty, questions that force doubt, questions that evoke the pained admission that belief sometimes seems a pale refuge indeed. Smug faith is not faith. True faith is tortured by the inability to make sense of this world and by a recognition that no single creed will wash away the scars of human anguish or definitively answer the promptings of the human heart and mind confronted by an often unforgiving world.

Traditional sources speak to this problem with a variety of voices. Even within the ambit of a single faith, the Jewish faith, no certain answer has been found, and it seems unlikely that a single, satisfactory answer ever will be. Of course, the admission of insufficiency is not the same as the admission of total failure. There is a measure of comfort and reassurance to be had within the framework of belief in a personal God, which should not be overlooked.

The Jewish tradition has approached evil in different ways, understanding that no single solution will feel valid in all the times and situations of life. Some of these profound attempts to reconcile a kind God with an often savage world are detailed below.

GOD IS GUILTY

No concept in Jewish thought illustrates so dramatically the intimacy between human beings and God as does the accusation of the Almighty. Throughout their history, Jews have not scrupled to take God to task for injustices, to accuse God of betraying His own standards of conduct.

The accusation of God has deep roots in Jewish history. The first terse and soaring example is Abraham, standing alone, defending the people of Sodom, to whom he has no connection save that they are his fellow human beings. Upon being told that God is planning to destroy the city, Abraham begins what is surely the most presumptuous round of bargaining on record, aiming to induce God to spare His wrath. In the midst of his wrangling with God, attempting to preserve the city, Abraham asks the biting rhetorical question "Shall the Judge of all the earth not do justice?" (Gen. 18:25)

Abraham's audacity still surprises a reader of the biblical story. How dare he, this ephemeral creature of flesh and blood, presume to challenge the decree of the Author and Sovereign of the universe? Is not Abraham obligated to accept, without reservation or questioning, the decrees of God who is, as Abraham himself acknowledges, the ultimate Judge?

To put the question that way misses the central point about the accusation of God. God Himself is seen as the Author of standards that human beings are to uphold. As He is kind, compassionate, just, merciful, so must they be kind, compassionate, just, merciful. Only by internalizing those standards, by making them their own, can people fashion a more just world. To assume that we may not question God is to assume that we have no real handle on what is good. Since all of religion presupposes that we have some knowledge of the good, we have the right to hold the Author of ethical norms to those same norms Himself. God cannot escape His own pronouncements. He is Judge of all the earth. He must do justice.

The posture of accusation does not end with Abraham. What the patriarch began is a continuing and vital strand of Jewish reaction to evil. The Psalmist, in embittered fury, cried out centuries later:

> *Rouse Yourself; why do You sleep, O Lord?*
> *Awaken, do not reject us forever!*
> *Why do You hide Your face,*
> *Ignoring our affliction and distress?*
>
> (Ps. 44:24–25)

The helpless anguish of the believer is full to overflowing. How can it be that God is asleep? Why does God not look on the carnage and savagery that reigns below? The accusation of God seems often to take the interrogative form; the question mark is eloquent—it presumes that there is an answer but it is being withheld. God, there must be a reason why Your actions are so brutal. Tell us. We can wait no longer. "How long, O Lord, shall I cry out, and You not listen, shall I shout to You 'Violence!' and You not save?" (Habakkuk 1:2).

Presuming moral authority over God is ennobling to human beings. It grants at least the dignity of the sufferer to reprimand. It offers an outlet for some of the anger and indignation that seizes the person unjustly made to suffer. Although in the midst of pain, which is itself debilitating and even humiliating, one has the right to challenge God.

Protest never ceased in the Jewish tradition. In the book of Job, it is the animating force—the idea that a righteous individual can insist upon the injustice of his situation and demand some sort of explanation. The book of Job, as we recall, is built around a seemingly simple theme. Job is an individual of undoubted righteousness; both the narrator and the voice of God in the book insist that Job is "blameless and upright" (1:1, 8). Nonetheless, he suffers a devastating series of catastrophes, losing his possessions, his children, his health, in rapid succession. The drama of the book is largely Job's reaction. Will he, as predicted, curse God? Will he meekly submit?

As we know, Job fires volley after poetic volley of accusation and anger at God. Bewailing his own misfortune, lamenting the day he was ever born, Job also insists that God has wronged him. He wishes, in a marvelous metaphor, that he could bring God up on charges in a court of law (9:2–5, 15–20). Job retains the integrity of his perception. He will not relent and simply "admit," as his friends advise, that he has done something wrong. Rather, Job maintains, *he* has been wronged.

In passages of undeniable power, Job rebukes God for injustice. "Know that God has wronged me; He has thrown up siege works around me. . . . He kindles His anger against me; He regards me as one of His foes" (19:6, 11). Job cannot be persuaded to admit wrong when he knows he is innocent: "By God who has deprived me of justice, who has embittered my life, as long as there is life in me . . . my lips will speak no wrong. . . . Until I die I will maintain my integrity" (27:2–5).

If readers did not instinctively feel that Job has the right to accuse God, the book would sacrifice much of its poetic power and emotive force. Job matters because accusing God of injustice is a serious, permissible, and even inevitable business.

Job also matters because he stakes out the most difficult position, one that Jews in the generations to follow will also grasp: he will believe but not without questions. Job does not lose his faith. Dismissing the possibility of a just God would certainly dissolve the problem. But Job clings to the horns of the dilemma: God exists and is good and he, Job, has done nothing wrong and yet is being punished. Until the very end of the book and the revelation of God's presence, Job insists upon the propriety of his question. For millennia, Jews have followed this tightrope of infuriated faith.

The assault on God in the Jewish tradition can be vicious in the pungency of its rhetoric. The author of Lamentations, having witnessed the exile, sees God as a bear or lion, lying in wait to destroy him (3:5). God stops up his prayer, makes him desolate, fills him with bitterness, actually shatters his bones and pierces him with arrows. The description of God's activity is quite explicit—He acts like an enemy. "I thought: 'My strength and my hope had perished before the Lord' " (3:18). The author of Lamentations understands quite well that the first obligation of the believer who has been betrayed is rage.

The elevation of anger as a theological response is carried on by the Rabbis. As we might expect, part of the Rabbinic attempt to cope with the problem of evil in this world is a pained outcry against the God who permits it to occur. In a daring twist on the verse in Exodus "Who is like You [God] among the mighty [Elim]," the Rabbis ask, "Who is like you among the dumb [Illemim]? Who like you hears the humiliation of His children and remains silent?" (Gittin 56b) The silence of God in the face of suffering stands as an unassimilable part of human experience, a persistent pain that cannot be soothed. Bitter sarcasm against God escapes Rabbi Abba Hanan as he comments on the ninth verse in Psalm 89: " 'O Lord, God of hosts, who is mighty like You?' You are mighty in that You hear the blaspheming and reviling and insults of that wicked man [the Roman general Titus] and still restrain Yourself!" (Gittin, 56b)

Theologically, such mocking of God's power is perilously close to plain blasphemy. It takes enormous courage for a religious individual to strike out so boldly, and yet the very paradigms of Jewish faith, the Rabbis of the Talmud, wield an almost Swiftian satire against God. This is not only another, and particularly striking, example of the closeness of the Divine-human relationship. It is a tribute to the Rabbis' honesty.

Protest does not answer the question of evil, but it helps maintain the sanity of the accuser. Indignation allows the

Jew to preserve the integrity of his or her own perception. It is not a matter of being so blind that we believe, ultimately, that all is just, and we should therefore meekly submit. Intellectual and moral courage is critical. Blunting our own faculties and sense of criticism is not the answer. It is a simple tribute to honesty of observation when the Rabbis comment that God seems often to be asleep in this world (M. Ps. 59:5). In the following Midrash, the Rabbis make even clearer how important it is for one to be true to one's own perception of God:

> Moses initially described God to the people as: "The great God, the mighty, the awesome" (Deut. 10:17). Later Jeremiah saw that strangers were destroying God's Temple. How then could God be termed "awesome"? So he omitted the word "awesome" [from his prayer to God, Jer. 32:17ff.]. Still later, Daniel saw that strangers enslaved God's children. Where then are God's "mighty" deeds? So he omitted the word "mighty" [in his prayer, Daniel 9:4ff.]. (Yoma, 69b)

To Jeremiah, God did not, at that moment, seem awesome. To Daniel, he did not seem mighty. Rather than paper over such "heretical" perceptions, the Rabbis highlight them. Each prophet, each person, must honestly evaluate the appearance of God in his or her own time and life. That this will evoke anger is to be expected and respected. Anger has a long and noble pedigree in Judaism, directed against a God who so often seems less protective, less good, than we have been promised.

Protest, however, always takes place in a Jewish context. One cannot pound fists and scream against some abstract entity with whom one has not entered into relationship. Human beings can be angry at God because human beings and God are close, because they have a mutual debt, and stand with each other in this world. Erase that relationship, dissolve the bonds of mutual responsibility embodied in covenant and there is no sense nor poignancy to human anger against God.

Remarkable in this respect is the tale reported by Solomon ibn Verga, a Jew who survived the Spanish Inquisition. Jews from all over Spain were forced to convert or be banished. Many chose banishment and set out on terrible, often fatal journeys. In Verga's work *Shevet Yehuda* he tells the stories of many who suffered and some who survived. In one tale, he reports on a man who, having endured a harrowing voyage at sea, landed together with his wife and two children and set out to find a place to live. After a long, excruciating trek, the woman weakened and died. Grief-stricken but undaunted, the husband carried his two children until all three of them fainted from weakness and hunger. Upon awakening, he discovered that his children too had died.

In his anguish, he stood up and said: "O Lord of the world, You are trying desperately to force me to abandon my faith in You. You will not prevail. Even against Your own will, I shall remain faithful." With that, he buried his children and continued his search for a new home.

The Jewish fury at God is not the vilification of an alien and hostile force. It is the distress and disappointment of being wounded by someone close. The Jews and God are locked in a lover's quarrel. Out of it is born the rich theme of protest and accusation against the One who represents ultimate justice. Israel wishes to be comforted by God, but we are told in the Midrash Israel will accept no comforting from God until they rebuke Him for His conduct (Pes. R. 30:4). God will accept the reproof and admit He "acted foolishly" with Israel. Only then, having registered the protest and received their apology, will Israel relent and accept consolation.

THE SUFFERING OF GOD

Intellectual history can sometimes resemble a trading floor, where ideas become the property of this or that group, often without reference to the previous owner. When they are presented again, they appear as strangers to those who once owned them. So it is with the subject of this section. For most Jews, the notion that God suffers seems profoundly Christian. Indeed, it stands at the very center of Christian theology in the image of Jesus upon the cross. But it is an idea with deep Jewish roots, and its resonance for Christians should not deprive Jews of the opportunity of exploring its impact upon Judaism and Jewish life.

The concept of a God who is Himself pained by the sufferings of His children is a powerful and rich idea. Not surprisingly, it is found in abundance in the Midrash. "How can we prove that when even one individual suffers God too is afflicted? It is proved by the verse in the Psalms (91:15): 'When he calls on Me, I will answer him; I will be with him in distress; I will rescue him and make him honored' " (S.E.R. 18).

No injustice in this world is suffered alone. No matter how quiet or hidden the suffering, how silent the afflicted, there is One who not only knows of it, but likewise feels the pain. There are lives of quiet desperation, but no lives of solitary desperation, for all suffering is shared. This is the critical insight of the Midrash, and one that has enormous implications for how human beings feel about the suffering that is the inevitable lot of all.

The Midrash is graphic in its depiction of God's suffering, teaching that God clasps His hands over His heart and weeps for the tragedies that have befallen Israel (S.E.R. 17). This image, elaborated upon below, is deeply rooted in the Rabbinic approach to God. For if God is caring, then He cannot be indifferent to the sufferings of His creations.

No attempt is made in Rabbinic literature to elaborate systematically the insight that God suffers. At many points in such descriptions (as in anthropomorphic descriptions generally) the Rabbis avail themselves of the word *kivyachol,* meaning "as it were" or "so to speak." So the Midrash reads in one place: "When one of His creatures is troubled God, as it were, is troubled too" (Tanh., Acharay). This linguistic equivocation guards against the accusation that the Rabbis are turning God into a human being. Of course, such a charge misses the point. A God who is caring, as the Rabbis considered God must be, has to feel the distress of human beings. Precisely how this comes about they cannot say. Still, that is how it must be.

The suffering of God is given in more explicit and moving terms in many Midrashim that speak not only about God's suffering, but about His weeping. In the innermost recesses, we are told, God weeps (Hag. 5b). He weeps day and night for the destruction of the Temple (Pes. R. 29:2).

God's weeping is in part due to His frustrated expectations for His children, a sort of parental cry: "God weeps over the failings of His creatures" (Hag. 5b). Part of the pain of being God is witnessing the mess that His creations have made of this world. The Bible records God's disillusionment with His creation in the story of the flood (Gen. 6:6), and His attempts to come to terms with the imperfections that must necessarily mar His effort. It is no more than an extrapolation of such tales in the Bible to see God as suffering with, and because of, His creations. Jeremiah 13:17 reads: "For if you will not give heed, My inmost self must weep, because of your arrogance; My eye must stream and flow with copious tears because the flock of the Lord is taken captive." God weeps not only for the pain of His creatures, but for the insensitivity and inhumanity of his creatures. While God cries in sorrow for the persecuted, He weeps as well, in frustration and disappointment, for the persecutors.

God does care and feel pain for the wicked as well as for the good. This remarkably liberal conclusion is illustrated by several Midrashim. "Even," declares God, "when the people are rebellious, I do not abandon them" (Ex. R. 33:2). More dramatically, although God felt compelled to bring a flood upon the world in the time of Noah because the world had become thoroughly corrupt and contemptible, He mourned for seven days before the flood (Gen. R. 27:4). And perhaps most famous and significant is God's rebuke to the angels who begin to sing a hymn of triumph as the sea closes over the Egyptians. "How can you sing," cries God, "while My creations are drowning?" (San. 39b)

God weeps for many reasons, particularly the terrible destruction wreaked by human beings and their callousness toward each other. In a series of vignettes based upon the verse "For these things I weep" (Lamentations 1:16), the Rabbis enumerate various historical tragedies. Following each graphic recounting of slaughter, the voice of God cries out, "For these things I weep" (Lam. R. 1:45ff.).

The sorrow and suffering of God is a powerful idea. It universalizes the human tragedy of suffering and makes it cosmic in scope and importance. Nonetheless, it cannot be a full answer to the problem of suffering. To suffer with someone is better than to suffer alone, but it is better still to be spared. Companionship is not an antidote to pain, and even the greater closeness that common trouble sometimes brings is hardly a sufficient warrant to be glad of tragedy.

Still, an empathic God, One who is afflicted, who weeps, is perhaps the most vivid image of the intimacy that reigns between the Jew and God. The bond of the people is fast and unbroken. A Midrash on a verse in Psalms (91:15) imagines it as follows: As with twins, one feels the other's ache; so God feels the pains of Israel (Ex. R. 2:5). This is a relationship of intimacy that cannot be effaced even by the agonies that sometimes drive human beings from their relationship with God.

Seemingly, God is made very human by this idea, but not if it is viewed in proper context. What it means for God to suffer we can never truly know. Clearly the tradition does not conceive of it as analogous to human suffering, because Judaism has ever been unequivocal in its insistence that God is not human. Where intellectual faculties fail, the heart must have its say. Understanding what it means for God to suffer is less important than the vivid beauty of the image: a God involved in human life and death such that He will feel its tragedies, weep for its pain.

The Midrashic God mourns just as do human beings: sitting in sackcloth, weeping, walking barefoot (Lam. R. 1:1). Perhaps most poignantly, God reverses the famous verse in Isaiah " 'Comfort, oh comfort My people,' says your God" (40:1) to a plea that the people assuage His pain: "Comfort Me, comfort Me O My people" (Pes. de-R.K., 16:9). God is not only suffering, but turns to human beings as they so often turn to Him, to salve the wounds of this world. More than once in the Midrash we find the lovely idea that human beings have it in their power to comfort God.

Such Midrashim teach us anew that the God of Judaism is anything but the stern and forbidding God of popular portrayal. Rather, between God and people there is a commonality of standards, interests, even of pain. Although this will certainly not solve the dilemma of human suffering, it is important for the believer to feel that God cares. This is an assurance that the Midrash poignantly affords.

Reb Levi Yitzhak of Bereditchev, one of the greatest of the Chasidic Rabbis, once said, "Dear God, I care not why I suffer. I wish only to know that I suffer for Your sake." We might say, looking into the roots of the Jewish tradition: "Dear God, I care not so much why I suffer. I wish only to know that You share my pain."

MORAL DRAMA

From a theistic viewpoint, the most common answer to the problem of evil is that God granted human beings free will, and it is this free will that determines their actions. Much of our blame of God is misdirected—we should blame ourselves for the chaos and the agony we have wrought on this globe.

To ask why God does not step in and change the course of history is to ask why God does not reduce humanity to puppets and end the world as we know it. If we would be human, we must bear the inevitable consequence—the ability to be inhuman. We cannot ask God to correct our mistakes, wipe the slate clean, and begin anew each time we err.

That argument makes sense as far as it goes, but it has long been recognized that it is not enough. For there are catastrophes we have not made and cannot stop, such as disease and natural disaster. Even were all human wickedness to be blamed upon us alone (and that too can be questioned, for we did not fashion human nature), there is still a large residue of suffering that is certainly not the fault of humanity.

Some will urge an additional argument at this point to buttress the "free will" defense. If the world is truly, as religion teaches, a moral drama in which all are supposed to learn to love the good, then there must be a certain amount of undeserved suffering. If we were all rewarded for our good deeds, there would be no merit in being good. We would choose the good in order to gain our reward. Like the child who refuses to steal a cookie because he knows punishment will follow, we would act appropriately for fear of being punished. Retribution, were it predictable, would erase any element of personal striving for good, since it would be pure self-interest that motivated proper action. Religion seeks a higher ideal.

"Do not be," taught Antigonus of Socho, "like servants who perform the will of your master for a reward" (Pirke Avoth, 1:3). Evil, undeserved evil, ensures disinterested goodness is done, for none can be certain of reward in this world, so if one is good, it is ultimately for its own sake.

The upshot of such reasoning is that all suffering, however powerfully personal it feels, is part of a greater scheme, to refine in the fire of pain the souls of humanity. We must suffer disproportionately to what we deserve, for in that way we will learn goodness.

There is sense in this argument, but it cannot carry against the endless sufferings of history. Tears have run too freely, too many lives have been destroyed without even the chance to have taken part in this "moral drama," for us to feel warm comfort from the possibility. As a point in theological debate it can perhaps carry. Yet it will not exonerate the kind of God about whom we speak, One fired with compassion, who feels with His creatures, whose decisions are both just and kind. Even the most powerful promptings of abstract argument melt away when confronted with the heat of human anguish. The practice of theodicy, the attempt to justify God in an evil world, is an enterprise whose rules are written by the sufferers of history and not by its logicians.

ESCHATOLOGY

Eschatology refers to the "end of days," and in this section we will consider several related areas often mentioned with reference to suffering: life after death, the Messiah, resurrection.

Contrary to what many believe, Judaism affirms a life after death. Though the fate of the individual after death is almost ignored in the Bible, the Rabbis frequently speak of *olam habah,* the world to come. Their assumption was that this life is not all, that there is a continuation of existence, although its precise nature and status are a mystery to us.

Whether a belief in such doctrines, be they messianic, resurrectional, or of the existence of a soul after death, is still available to us is a question. Skepticism about the claims of messianists is not new. As long as there have been promises there have also been disappointments. It is also true that as long as there have been disappointments there have been renewed hopes.

What matters here is not the plausibility of the belief, but whether the existence of life after death can provide the much-sought-after "answer" to suffering. Is the promise of a reward adequate compensation for the ills of earth?

It cannot be, even for those who have faith that this life is not all. Suffering once felt cannot be erased. Life cut off early is never restored, no matter what other delights may or may not hold in the future. The mathematics of reward and punishment are not convincing. What possible recompense could there be that would permit us to feel that an innocent individual should have been racked by pain in this world?

Belief in life after death is some compensation, and in the elaborate descriptions of bliss in the future, we may detect an attempt to redress the earthly balance. A sad and revealing example of this is the Midrashic statement that God conducts classes in the heavenly academy for children who died too early to learn His word here on earth (A.Z. 3b). The picture is lovely, but behind it is the inescapable realization that there is no compensation for having been cut off from life in youth.

Dignity is due the sufferers, and we deprive them of this by too-easy equations that validate the necessity of their pain. To say one had to suffer is to take away the legitimacy of the accusation that Judaism supports. You may not deny the right of another to feel wronged, wounded, angered by the hand life has dealt. Some pains are too deep to salve and too inexplicably awful to pretend they have explanation.

IT IS NOT IN OUR HANDS

The final theme is the hardest to accept and the least avoidable. For it involves a simple choice, one of the inescapable decisions we would rather skirt or ignore. There is no real middle ground between believing that there is a God and rejecting Him on the basis of the evil in the world. Sooner or later one must make what contemporary philosophers are pleased to call an existential choice.

Ultimately no answer to the problem of evil and God satisfies. Some are helpful, but we are in the end forced back on the possibility that the true or final answer eludes our grasp. "It is not in our hands," laments Rabbi Yannai, "to explain either the prosperity of the wicked or even the sufferings of the just" (Pirke Avoth 4:19). In this life, that may have to remain the final word. Centuries of tortured ingenuity and deep-souled inquiry have not produced a more conclusive or comprehensive response.

In the aftermath of the Holocaust, in the darkness that descended on our century, the question has been grappled with anew. Although the Holocaust yielded both deeper doubts and stories of unbelievable sturdiness of faith, we cannot say that we have formulated new answers. Indeed, more than any event in Jewish history it is the destruction of one-third of the Jewish people that forces upon us the painful truth that there can be no adequate answers. Behind the barbed wire, in the shadow of the gas chambers, all answers sound like mockery.

Still, many who were there, and many who have thought deeply and seriously about the events of our time, have emerged with faith. But if a choice is taken for faith, it matters very much what kind of faith. What the discussion above emphasizes is that even in the context of the most difficult and alienating of theological issues, that of evil, the Rabbis operated in the context of a personal God and of closeness to that God. The answer that was *not* given is as significant as that which was. We must listen, if we wish to know the essence of another's views, for the position left unstated. And the one answer that was not offered by the Talmudic Rabbis is that God is indifferent. That was not possible. God cares, passionately, deeply, enough to be moved, enough to listen to human protestations, enough to cry.

The possibility of unbelief was well known to the Rabbis. They knew quite well, for example, of systems where there were good and bad deities in the world, and some of the non-Jewish thinkers with whom they came into contact even accused the biblical God of being an evil Deity. Still, the certainty of God's mercies never deserted them, even in the most difficult times. That God did not exist or was unjust could never be the Rabbinic response.

The problems of this world, when viewed from a certain angle, may even be seen as a demonstration of God's concern. Divinity is seen not only in interconnectedness, but in insufficiency, in the room left for human beings to create, to explore, to err. Commenting on one of the biblical names for God, *El Shaddai,* the Talmudic sage Resh Lakish said,

"El Shaddai—I am the one who said to the world, '*Dai!*' "—enough! That is, God is not only the One who created, but the One who *stopped* creation—did not provide everything or solve all (Hag. 12a and Torah T'mimah, Gen. 17:1). El Shaddai is a God who was trusting enough to leave us room for creative achievement and horrible mistakes, a God who loved enough to leave spaces.

That is part of the beauty of the Kabbalistic idea of tsimtsum detailed above, that God retracted to make room for the world to be created. Like a parent who must relent to allow his or her children room to grow, God abdicated part of His control to human freedom and willfulness. Any parent must let go from love, however agonizing the consequences can be.

Yet the refusal to intervene has been a source of fury and frustration for as long as men and women have shaken fists at the sky and cursed fate. Isaiah long ago cried out, after the destruction of the Temple, "Our holy Temple, our pride, where our ancestors praised You, has been consumed by fire, and all that was dear to us is ruined. At such things will You restrain Yourself, O Lord? Will You stand idly by and let us suffer so greatly?" (Is. 64:10–11) We have not advanced much beyond the prophet's uncomprehending anger.

All these explorations are tentative and partial. The clamor for justice in our hearts rings nearly as loud as the clamor to be remembered. That the world is unjust seems the single sustained assurance of history. That human beings, glorious and murderous, demigods who damn each other to indescribable tortures, should one day create justice on their own defies belief and invites the coercive visions of the half mad. Sometimes we feel moved to believe in God simply because, although the justice of God has not shown itself in our history, we know the only absolute justice is ultimate. If there is no God, justice is a poor patched thing indeed.

A Jewish legend holds that redemption will come when the tears of the Jewish people have filled a giant vat in heaven. Surely even the authors of that sentiment, centuries ago, must have marveled at the dimensions of a vat so vast as to contain the tears shed by the Jewish people in that oppressive age. Yet what is significant about the legend is not only the redemptive hope. It is the essential symbolism—tears are measured. Barring salvation, the greatest hope is that cries are heard, that human agony is not a tiny, pitiful squeal to an indifferent cosmos, but has the dignity of true outcry—it is listened to.

No one will imagine that this discussion has attained the answer we seek. For the religious individual, as important as the answer is the realization that the search is authentic and legitimate, that one may be true to the experience of this world and remain in the context of belief. Also important is the realization that each position carries tremendous difficulties. For the nonbeliever, there is no reason to expect justice, and so no anguished searching for the cause of its absence. But that is still to live in an unjust world, only without hope that there is a source of ultimate justice that may one day make it right. Both positions have their pains and heartache.

The Rabbis felt an assurance that God's message would survive despite suffering, despite death. The martyrdom of Rabbi Hananiah ben Teradyon, a second-century sage, makes this point hauntingly. Under penalty of death, he continued to teach Torah. When he was captured, the Romans wrapped a Torah scroll around him and set him on fire, placing moist wool over his heart to slow the flames and prolong his agony. His students, gathered around to watch the terrible final moments of their beloved teacher, asked, "Rabbi, what do you see?" Hananiah ben Teradyon answered, "The parchment is burning, but the words are ascending to heaven" (A.Z. 18a).

Evil can destroy; the parchment burned. But it cannot triumph, for the words survived.

Equally important to the question of evil, as this story demonstrates, is the response we choose. We can passively acquiesce, or choose to fight evil in the world. Judaism insists that, although evil in this world may be unexplained, it cannot go unchallenged. Though there be no solution, there must be a response. "Justice, justice shall you pursue," commands the Bible (Deut. 16:20), and equal with the admonition is the reason, "that you may live. . . ." Human society becomes impossible without reaction to evil, without the sustained attempt to combat that which cannot be erased but might, with our best efforts, be subdued.

We must grant the final word in this section to Levi Yitzhak of Bereditchev, the Chasidic Rabbi mentioned above. A story is told of him that once, right before the Kol Nidre service, the opening service of the Day of Atonement, he stood before the ark as the sun was about to set. For a long time he stood, silent, still, as the evening approached. Noticing that the time to begin prayer was upon them, his students and disciples became uncomfortable, worrying that the Rabbi would begin too late. At the last possible moment, he spoke.

"Dear God," he said, "we come before You this year, as we do every year, to ask Your forgiveness. But in this past year, I have caused no death. I have brought no plagues upon the world, no earthquakes, no floods. I have made no women widows, no children orphans. God, You have done these things, not me! Perhaps You should be asking forgiveness from me."

The great Rabbi paused, and continued in a softer voice. "But, since You are God, and I am only Levi Yitzhak, *Yisgadal v'yiskadah sh'mei rabah*," and he began the service.

That is the final answer. There is no escaping the pain of suffering and the tormenting questions of God's silence. In the end, however, the Jewish position has always been to understand that, however close, there is a gap between human beings and God, and we cannot finally understand His intentions or design.

Therefore we continue to pray.

9

Arrival: The Healer of Shattered Hearts

> Rabbi Alexandri said: "If a person uses broken vessels, it is considered an embarrassment. But God seeks out broken vessels for His use, as it says: 'God is the healer of shattered hearts.'"
>
> —Leviticus Rabbah 7:2

Succinctly and for all time, the anguished Job stated the problem of humanity: "My days fly faster than a weaver's shuttle and come to their end" (Job 7:6). Life rolls downhill, picking up speed with each passing year. When it becomes clear, at different ages for different individuals, that life will one day end, we all search for permanence and place ourselves on the uniquely human torture rack—the one that insists that we must leave something of ourselves although we know full well that all we are will disappear.

The problem is as old as mortality, which is as old as humanity. We can understand, then, why the urge to live itself becomes at times more important, more imperative, than living for a particular purpose; why success can override worth. If seeking to leave a mark is so compelling, the particular type of mark begins to lose importance, and its very presence, often in the form of fame or success, takes precedence.

Part of the peculiar mania of our society is that success by itself, of any kind, is revered. The skill of steering a motorcycle over several buses, in itself both worthless and recklessly dangerous, is venerated when done *successfully*. A level of skill is reckoned to be its own accomplishment. "I don't care what you do, so long as you do it well" goes the thoughtless platitude, carrying in its smooth wake some awful implications. But it does matter what you do, in addition to how well you do it. The less skillful the killer, the better. Many times in history we might have wished for less competence: the world would be a better place had the horrific engine of the Nazi machine been less well oiled. The enormous success of tyrannical ideologies around the globe gives one pause to realize that success by itself is no criterion of admiration or value.

In Rabbinic literature there is the interesting statement that Bilaam, the Moabite sorcerer who tried to curse Israel, was as great in prophetic powers as Moses. Some even claim that Bilaam's visionary capacities were the greater of the two (S.E.R. 26). Given the Rabbinic veneration of the power and personality of Moses, it is no small surprise that this figurehead of the Jewish people should be compared (and unfavorably at that!) with a pagan prophet. The comparison serves to underscore the Jewish attitude toward ability—its misuse is more heinous than its absence. To have power is a marvelous thing. Without it there is no hope of affecting events in this world and righting injustices, which is the aim of the Jewish ideal, tikkun olam, repairing the world. To worship power for its own sake, however, or its relatives success, wealth, beauty (all of which are permutations of power), is idolatry, and of a very destructive kind.

Renouncing the worship of power has always been difficult. Humanity, weak and uncertain, will seek models of strength. It is this fear of trusting our own unaided energies and faculties (which arises from the very sensible realization that the world is too much to handle alone) that drives us to invest others with almost magical faculties to cure our ills or save our selves. We venerate power because our own weakness scares us, because we feel frail inside, because we grasp gratefully on to someone who seems capable of shouldering the burdens that appear simply overwhelming. To see another exercise mastery has talismanic force, mesmerizing us. The resultant spell is often more than a healthy esteem; it is the uncritical and destructive worship of people.

Seductions of success will never be erased. They can be mitigated, however, and grounded on more solid foundations if we maintain a sense of what success is praiseworthy and what is merely self-aggrandizing or even perilous. The successes of poisonous ideologies should win not our adoration but our scorn and resolute opposition. The accumulation of wealth by rapacity and callousness should arouse not our admiration but our contempt. Wealth is an opportunity, a marvelous one, to redress the inequities that flourish in human society. As with all forms of power, it is a means, not an end. It can be aimless as well as grand, destructive as easily as generative. The value, the end, the higher vision, determines its worth.

The Rabbis point out that in the account of the golden calf, the idol that the children of Israel built in the desert, the people contributed their "golden earrings" to Aaron to help with the construction. Later, that same people, the erring ancient Israelites, contributed their "golden earrings" to the construction of the tabernacle (Ex. R. 48:6). Identical means may serve wildly divergent ends. Wealth, like every human commodity, can be used to worship idols or to serve God.

The same may be said of all human qualities. "When I was young I used to admire intelligent people," said A. J. Heschel, "as I grow older I admire kind people." Intellectual acumen is a wonderful thing, but it often serves as an excuse for boorishness, condescension, and indifference, as though the granting of brain power were somehow a certificate of a higher humanity. Unfettered intelligence has done great harm in this world, and were professions to be called, one by one, to the bar of history, the intellectual pursuits would have a great deal to answer for.

This is not a novel observation, nor a particularly surprising one. Such emphases have been the cry of moralists for ages. We all realize this to be true on some level, and yet we are seduced, again and again, to proffer our admiration to the undeserving. Why is the backsliding so certain, so predictably human? Part of it must be simple thoughtlessness. It also reflects a certain immaturity, or at least inexperience. Yet on another level it suggests again the possibility of a missing relationship with God.

Reverence is a human capacity and need. For much of this book we have described individuals as haunted by fears, uncertain, often unstable. The fragility of our lives, the uncertainty of our perceptions, leads us to search for that which is stronger than ourselves. The allegiance of human beings can be very strong, and very sure. A personality of power captures hearts, wins loyalty, because for a moment we bask in the glow of greater strength, in the illusion that some human creature has escaped the gnawing instability that shadows our own lives. Throughout history, people have thrown their hearts to others who seem possessed of an inexplicable magic, a greater grace, what we often call charisma. We all feel the need to be saved. Often the savior appears to be the untouched one, the serene and powerful person beside or before us.

The need of worship is real for all people. He who does not worship God will find something else to worship—material goods, power, or perhaps other human beings. "Even an atheist," wrote the philosopher Walter Kaufmann, "needs a sense of blasphemy." He might as easily have remarked that even an atheist has a sense of worship, and will worship somehow. Humanity cannot live without reverence. How worthy is that which we worship? That is one crucial test for any life. Do we revere ourselves, the work of our hands? The Talmud tells the tale of two men walking past the ruins of an ancient synagogue. One of them, saddened by the desolate rubble, sighs and remarks, "How much money have my ancestors invested here!" His friend gently rebukes him: "How many *souls* have your ancestors invested here?" (P. T. Peah 8:9) The question is not the splendor of what we have built, but why we built it, what we invested of our souls. Do we create for a higher purpose? Can we conceive of anything greater than ourselves? Is there in our veneration a degree of recognition that we are mortal creations of God?

There is a deeper theme implicit in wrongheaded worship. It is that we make the rules, the values, and estimate their worth. Moral laws can come from only one of two sources: human beings or God. If we are the authors of moral law, then it all depends upon what we think, and that may change with time and circumstance. In one society, murder may seem appropriate. If I think something is impressive, it matters not that some overscrupulous moralist thinks it unworthy of esteem, for we are both people, and we have a simple difference of opinion. If each is inventing his or her own standards, no one's is better than anyone else's, they are just different. Only if the rules are beyond us, Divinely authored, can we escape the perils of "opinion ethics." The contagion of relativism (like its mirror image absolutism) presents a serious threat to the true complexity of moral thought. Total relativism will not admit of value beyond ourselves. Absolutism will not admit of the value in our selves to challenge and differ. No illusions have wreaked greater havoc in our time.

Fanaticism is not a new disease. The Talmud relates that after the rebellion against the Romans, the great mystic

Rabbi Simeon bar Yochai emerged from years of hiding in a remote cave. Upon first stepping into the sunlight, the Rabbi saw men working the fields. Angered at the sight of daily life proceeding normally when he had been praying and meditating in secret for so long, he exclaimed: "They forsake eternity and spend their time on transitory things!" Wherever he looked, the legend relates, the land was instantly consumed with flames. A voice came from heaven and said: "Have you come out of hiding in order to destroy My world? If so, go back to your cave" (Shab. 33b). This is not only a warning against fanaticism, it is an endorsement of the importance of daily life and everyday activities. They are more exalted than the righteous indignation of the great sage. Secluding oneself in a cave and meditating is not life. Working the field is life. Allowing others the dignity of different views is holy.

That there is no monopoly on truth does not mean, however, that there is no truth. We are in equal danger from those who believe that their morality is certain and unchallengeable and those who believe no morality can be certain. The seductive trap of extremes has poisoned the dialogue on both sides. Certain things must be reckoned right and others wrong or society collapses. Yet in order for there to be right and wrong in any higher sense, there must be a Divine authority.

Worship and value belong to God. That is the abstract, ideational premise upon which Jewish thought has, up to our own time, proceeded. As we have seen, however, when it stops with that there is a bloodless correctness to religion, which lacks the intimacy and spiritual depth that personal relationship can provide. For worship and value alone do not carry with them the urgency of intimacy, warmth, love.

We have seen repeatedly how the worship of God in the Jewish tradition is carried on in the context of closeness and devotion. Even in the most trying moments, the belief is affirmed that God cares for all His creations. This is beautifully illustrated by a famous tale told in the Talmud of Rabbi Meir and his pious, brilliant wife, Bruriah.

One Sabbath afternoon while Rabbi Meir was lecturing to his students, his two children succumbed to a long-standing illness. When Rabbi Meir returned home, Bruriah did not know how to tell him that his children had died. "Where are the children?" he asked. "I have a question for you," said his wife. "Ask it," replied Rabbi Meir. "I was once given a very valuable treasure to keep for someone. Today he came and claimed it. Should I return it to him?" Rabbi Meir replied that of course a deposit must be returned to its rightful owner. Bruriah led him gently up to the room where his children lay, and recited the verse from the book of Job: "The Lord has given, and the Lord has taken away; blessed be the name of the Lord" (1:21). They grieved and were comforted together (M. Prov. 31).

ZEALOTRY AND INDIFFERENCE

Sometimes God's advocates are His greatest foes. It is possible, as the sage Koheleth knew thousands of years ago, to be "righteous overmuch."

There are many whose devotion to God seems matched by a disregard for His creations, and the number seems sadly to be growing. Certainty and dogma take the place of thought and devotion. Assuming that all answers have been vouchsafed, they hold that we need only search the correct book or consult the appropriate authority and we will be gifted with an answer that cannot be questioned. Those who question do so, obviously, with evil intent. So runs the zealotry of our day, different in circumstance but not in kind from the zealotry of the ages.

Zealotry is actually a manifestation of human weakness.

In a tottering world, certain standards are eagerly sought, and the questioner, the one who upsets the standards, poses a threat to the smooth insularity of the constructed universe of the believer.

Those who preach an unyielding adherence to one standard or another should recall the wise words of Rabbi Israel of Rushin. He taught that while the Pentateuch consists of the *five* books of Moses, the classic code of Jewish law, the Shulchan Aruch, contains only four books. Why the discrepancy? Because the final part of the law is the person, who must himself complete and be counted in all religious activity. Too many who are wrapped up in texts, proscriptions, and prohibitions forget that most important "fifth book," the human being for which all religion is intended.

Significant as is this danger of zealotry, the greater danger for modern Jews is not zealotry but insufficient passion. The temptation to rob the God-Idea of its true depth and significance is great, because fervor appears inappropriate in our temperate times. So much damage has been done in this century by rabid devotion that we fear any glimpse of its countenance. We easily and rightly deplore zealotry. While such disapproval is surrounded by a vigorous chorus, the voice of legitimate passion about faith grows weak, and God's entry into human life is gradually, with moderation and liberality, closed.

There exists a middle way between indifference and fevered devotion. Judaism sees the path of history as the human dialogue with God. For the Rabbis, as we have seen, it can be rightly characterized as the dialogue of lovers. As with lovers, much has been said. Those who reject history and tradition ignore the generations of ideas, words, special moments that have passed between the lovers. Each close relationship develops its unique signals and memories, and to begin each conversation anew is needlessly impoverishing. However, to assume that all has already been said, that there are no new thoughts and ideas, that the possibilities are exhausted, is equally foolish. A dialogue means that there is much to listen to from the past and much to say about the future. The zealot who will countenance no innovation and the modern who rejects the cogency of past experience both make the mistake of losing part of the content of the conversation.

Dialogue should be ongoing in all areas and at all times of life. A God who is confined to specific ritual occasions, to the synagogue, to the occasional lecture, to the High Holidays, is not a God the Jewish tradition recognizes as its own. That God is kept so carefully compartmentalized is, in a way, a tribute to the force with which He can upset a life. For in fact, once the notion of God has broken free to accompany one's days, to walk by one's side, life appears in a different cast: not the amiable change promised by spiritual therapists who guarantee happiness and joy once God enters your life. The change is one of depth. It is a force to question and wonder. It is a call to notice that which usually escapes one's attention. To bring God closer in life is a challenge that is difficult to ignore, which is one reason why some prefer simply to avoid it.

As we have discussed, there are myriad other reasons for the absence of God in modern life. Honest belief in God is a taxing task in a scientific age in which we have seen so much tragedy—and so much more seems poised, prepared to strike. Genuine anguish, and the inability to view God as any sort of solution, is the condition of many. No theological formula will salve all wounds or quiet all doubts, nor should it. The task of those who tenuously but determinedly hold on to faith is to insist that God be seriously explored. For without faith we must necessarily search for substitutes, and though some may seem temporarily more credible than religious belief, they are not without dangers of their own.

The sociologist Philip Rieff coined the term "therapy of

commitment" to describe the many different approaches taken by our generation to express the undying need for some cause. For many, therapy itself is something to be committed to. The couch is not only a tool for cure, but an altar upon which faithless moderns can still feel the thrill of deep belief in something beyond themselves, in this case the psychological dogma and technique. Once we have lost the ability to throw our full faith into a single political dogma, and religion loses its force for us, personal transformation seems the only animating belief left to us. We can still change ourselves, and the possibility of reshaping the self becomes the grand article of faith.

None of the modern therapies of commitment are as transformative, however, as that of religious belief. None of them are as rooted in history, filled with the richness of ritual, with the trials and wisdom of thousands of years. Many modern therapies of commitment are enormously valuable and have greatly enhanced human life. They will not fill up the place of faith. We return again to Klatzkin's words: "God has no heir."

Judaism touches all facets of life. It proposes a meaning for history and for the solitary human existence. Outside of the bounds of peoplehood, faith—what has been termed the Jewish "civilization"—no other system will provide Jews with so comprehensive an approach to life, to each other, to themselves.

This book began with the question of God's centrality to Judaism. Many Jews have found their way to their tradition through different avenues—through communal work, through the arts, through scholarship. Judaism is large enough to contain many different types of devotion. Still, we know that like a living, changing organism, Judaism has a pulsing heart, that which gives it blood and life, the idea that stands at its core, and that is the idea of God.

The idea has been variously conceived, and it should not concern us if many of the depictions in this book are alien or uncomfortable. There is one God, but there is no one conception of Him. As the founder of Chasidism, the Baal Shem Tov, noted long ago, it is for a good reason that the Amidah prayer begins with the words "The God of Abraham, the God of Isaac, and the God of Jacob" instead of the more economical "The God of Abraham, Isaac, and Jacob." The repetition indicates that God appeared differently to each of the patriarchs. No single vision of God suffices for all.

In this age of spiritual search, it is well to recall that seeking is important, but it is not all. Finding counts, too. And although God is everywhere, there are certain places where the search will likely yield results. In the medieval poem *Ha-Melekh Ve-Ha Nazir,* Rabbi Abraham Halevy bar Hasdai wrote: "Where is God? In the heart of all who seek Him." Earnest and devotional pursuit of God is part of the Jewish tradition.

So is a God who needs to be pursued. In a passage of startling emotional urgency, God says to the people: "Why, when I came, was there no one there? Why, when I called, would none respond?" (Is. 50:2) Just as God is sought in the heart, He seeks the heart.

The answer to God's question was not entirely clear in the time of Isaiah, nor is it certain today. A catalog could be easily compiled of why faith has ebbed in our time. Many reasons have been discussed in these pages, and much more could be added. Whatever the reasons, skepticism has become the acceptable intellectual posture. We do not want to be fooled. We do not want to be credulous. We have been educated by advertising to doubt all claims, all bids for attention. The systematic attempt by so many to enlist our aid makes us shrink from devotion and into doubt.

There is a faith, however, hidden in honest doubt. Once,

when asked if his prayers that people be more charitable had been answered, a Chasidic Rabbi drolly remarked, "God answered half of my prayer: although the rich are not yet ready to give, the poor are ready to take." That is a realistic doubt that does not forget but questions, that will not allow the issue to die or be resolved. It is a doubt that gleams with faith. Indifference, not anguished denial, is the true enemy of faith, as the tradition has always known. Love does not die in hate, though it be horribly transfigured. Love dies in indifference. God may be spoken of with anger, dread, disappointment; He may be chided, challenged, argued with, accused; He may even be doubted with all the force of one's soul. We may look at the night sky and find it dumb. We may not stop looking, however, and that is the ultimate message of faith. The command to love God is paramount in Judaism because above all else God must be of constant concern.

The claims of spirit often bypass traditional religion. That is a shame, because the repository of centuries of spiritual insight lies in Judaism, although, as in any venture, in treasure hunting one must be educated in where and how to look. This book is one attempt to point the way to a source of spirit, to God, and suggest how He can be viewed, not with the dispassionate spectacles of bloodless philosophizing, but in the fire of personal commitment and devotion. The most renowned paragraph in the Jewish prayer service adjures us to love God. Without that love, the foundation of Judaism crumbles. More than that—without that love our lives can totter and so can the world we live in. Without it we seem to lack direction and soul.

We should not ask of God and of faith what they cannot do. God does not still the turbulence in our souls, ease all the paths of life, cup us in His hand and lay us gently on the other shore. God will not make our decisions. He will not reverse them when we have made decisions that are perilous, ominous, or wrong.

Faith will not alone make the world right. Faith cannot guarantee that its adherents will be good, unswayed by anger or hate, lost in a mist of kindness and prayer. Faith does not eradicate conflict or eliminate pain. It will not even promise always to stay the same inside the soul of the individual believer or the believing community.

But God can touch a life. Faith can alter vision. Little else in this polychrome world will suddenly pull things together, make the jagged pieces fall into place as will faith in God. Few things can go as far to ease the ache of loneliness, the terrible fear that we are spinning blindly through the universe. No other force can so fill the night with presence, hear the unspoken fears, calm the uncertain stirrings when the dark is so strong that even shadows disappear.

The Rabbis point out an interesting contrast in the biblical descriptions of Abraham and Noah. Of Noah, the Bible writes that he walked with God (Gen. 6:9). When speaking to Abraham, God enjoins him to "walk before Me" (Gen. 17:1). At first glance you might consider Noah to be the greater figure, since he walked *with* God. In fact, the Rabbis contend, the contrast is intended to be a compliment to Abraham. For Noah was like a small child who needed the support of his parent, and so walked with God so that he might not stumble and fall. But Abraham's strength was such that he could walk alone, unaided, with only the reassuring certainty that God was behind him (Tanh. B. Lech L'cha 26).

We are in many ways kin to the generation of Noah, the generation destroyed by the flood, for we live with the possibility of our own destruction. We have not followed Noah or Abraham, however, for we have walked independent of God, not with or before Him, confident that our own power and genius would be sufficient. Perhaps we are just now beginning to learn that, of all the options, to walk alone is the one the human race cannot afford, and cannot survive.

As individuals and as a society, we need to relearn the lesson of Noah. To learn anew how to walk with God, to have the strength to feel how weak we can be, and how much we are in need of guidance and of love. That learning is difficult. With all that we know and have seen, the confident assertions of this book may seem more wishful than realizable. Still, faith is not new, and its principal offer is to the struggle, not the certainty of finding. Many have for centuries found in it worth, meaning, help, and a sense of life well lived in a community of faith, in words of tradition, in actions and beliefs of ancient origin. The final bit of advice on the matter must be biblical, when God declares to humanity, "Come, let us reason together" (Is. 1:18). The offer, Judaism believes, still stands.

Perhaps one day, having learned to walk with God, we will be able to become a world on the model of Abraham, to take the burden of justice more squarely on our own shoulders, and to show that we have learned peace. Then we shall walk before God, and His presence will gaze from behind, still close, now proud.

Abbreviations

(in alphabetical order)

BIBLE

Deut.	Deuteronomy
Ex.	Exodus
Gen.	Genesis
Is.	Isaiah
Jer.	Jeremiah
Lev.	Leviticus
Num.	Numbers
Ps.	Psalms
Sam.	Samuel

RABBINIC WRITINGS

A.Z.	Avodah Zarah
Ber.	Berachot
B.M.	Bava Meziah
Deut. R.	Deuteronomy Rabbah
Eccl. R.	Ecclesiastes Rabbah
Ex. R.	Exodus Rabbah

Gen. R.	Genesis Rabbah
Hag.	Hagiga
Ket.	Ketubot
Kidd.	Kiddushin
Lam. R.	Lamentations Rabbah
Lev. R.	Leviticus Rabbah
Meg.	Megilla
M. HaG.	Midrash HaGadol
M. Prov.	Midrash Proverbs
M. Ps.	Midrash Psalms (Socher Tov)
Num. R.	Numbers Rabbah
Pes.	Pesachim
Pes. de-R.K.	Pesikta de-Rab Kahana
Pes. R.	Pesikta Rabbati
Pirke de-R.El.	Pirke de Rabbi Eliezer
P.T.	Palestinian Talmud
San.	Sanhedrin
S.E.R.	Seder Eliyahu Rabba
Shab.	Shabbat
Sifre Deut.	Sifre Deuteronomy
Sifre Num.	Sifre Numbers
Tanh.	Tanhuma
Tanh. B.	Tanhuma ed. Buber

Suggested Reading

This bibliography represents a small sampling of the books available. Many worthwhile and important works are not listed. Below I have tried to list books that are helpful to the general reader and deal with the topics covered in these pages. If a book is difficult to read, but nonetheless important to include, I have noted the difficulty. That still omits a great deal of territory, particularly biblical studies and the vast field of Jewish law.

Like everyone, I have my favorites, and some books are included not because they are better than all others in the field, but because they have touched me, or have a special place in my memory. I would like to single out two writers in particular who hold a place in my heart and are not that well known today. One is Maurice Samuel, whose books are unfailingly literate, witty, and important. He wrote many works, including *The Gentleman and the Jew* (New York: Alfred A. Knopf, 1950) and *Certain People of the Book* (New York: Alfred A. Knopf, 1955). A good selection of his work with a complete bibliography has been published as *The Worlds of Maurice Samuel,* edited by Milton Hindus, with a foreword by Cynthia Ozick (Philadelphia: Jewish Publication Society, 1977).

The other individual I would like to single out is Milton Steinberg, an American Rabbi who died at a tragically young age. All of his work is worthwhile, but in particular I want to call attention to his brief classic *Basic Judaism* (New York: Harcourt Brace, 1947), a sort of philosophical primer of Judaism's guiding principles, and the marvelous *As a Driven Leaf* (New York: Behrman House, 1939), the only novel Steinberg lived to write. *As a Driven Leaf* is a historical novel of Talmudic times that tells the story of Elisha ben Abuyah, the only Talmudic sage who abandoned Judaism and became a heretic. It is a penetrating examination of the problem of evil that makes the Rabbis come alive, and it is an important allegory for our time.

An additional note: Those books listed below with older publication dates are usually standards and have been reprinted many times.

1. INTRODUCTIONS

There are many introductions to Judaism, and a number of them are quite good. We will mention but a few of the many possibilities: Herman Wouk's *This Is My God* (New York: Doubleday, 1959) is an explanation of the major concepts, events, and practices of Judaism by an Orthodox Jew who has the advantage of being a novelist, and so knows how to write graceful prose. *Nine Questions People Ask About Judaism* by Dennis Prager and Joseph Telushkin (New York: Simon and Schuster, 1981) is a persuasive introduction that covers several compelling topics and puts Judaism in a broader societal and conceptual context. *The Way of Torah* by Jacob Neusner (Encino, Calif.: Dickenson Publishing Co., 1974) explains the classical ideas of Judaism, and the challenge of modernity. A brief introduction that approaches Judaism by its different streams of tradition (e.g., biblical, mystical, ethical, and so forth) is *Judaism* by Nicholas De Lange (Oxford, Eng.: Oxford University Press, 1986).

2. HISTORY

For a history of Talmudic times, one should look first in general Jewish histories, to get some sense of perspective on the sweep of Jewish history. Popular works abound, such as Chaim Potok's *Wanderings* (New York: Alfred A. Knopf, 1978), Paul Johnson's *History of the Jews* (New York: Harper and Row, 1987), and, although a bit less popular and more rigorous, *History of the Jewish People* by Max Margolis and Alexander Marx (Philadelphia: Jewish Publication Society, 1947). Finally, *Jewish People, Jewish Thought* by Robert M. Seltzer (New York: Macmillan, 1980) is a thorough and interesting survey of Jewish history with an emphasis on the ideas and events that contribute to Judaism today.

Three works that isolate the various epochs of Judaism are: *Great Ages and Ideas of the Jewish People,* edited by Leo W. Schwartz, with a contribution on the Rabbinic age by Gerson D. Cohen (New York: Random House, 1956); *The Jews: Their History, Culture and Religion* (Philadelphia: Jewish Publication Society, 1949), edited by Louis Finkelstein, with an essay on Rabbis and their age by Judah Goldin; and an outstanding one-volume history by a group of Israeli scholars, *A History of the Jewish People,* edited by H. H. Ben-Sasson (Cambridge, Mass.: Harvard University Press, 1976).

A standard, comprehensive work in the field is H. Graetz's six-volume *History of the Jews* (published in English by the Jewish Publication Society, Philadelphia, 1891–98). Although his work is understandably outdated in parts, it remains a classic text. More recent is the sixteen-volume work by Salo Baron, *A Social and Religious History of the Jews* (New York: Columbia University Press; and Philadelphia: Jewish Publication Society, 1952–76). Both have ample sections on Rabbinic times. For the period leading up to the Rabbinic age, *From the Maccabees to the Mishnah* by Shaye J. D. Cohen (Philadelphia: The Westminster Press, 1987) is a keen and reliable guide.

Important as well are E. Schurer's three-volume *The History of the Jewish People in the Age of Jesus Christ,* revised by G. Vermes and F. Millar (Edinburgh, 1973–86), and Jacob Neusner's *A History of the Jews of Babylonia,* in five volumes (Leiden: E. J. Brill, 1965–70). The principal lessons of this work are condensed in the same author's *There We Sat Down* (New York: Abingdon Press, 1972).

3. RABBINIC ANTHOLOGIES

Several works explain the theology of the Rabbis and contain liberal selections from their writings. For a clear and helpful selection, the reader might first try one of three works: Solomon Schechter, *Aspects of Rabbinic Theology* (New York: Schocken, 1961), which interweaves commentary and quotation; A. Cohen, *Everyman's Talmud* (New York: Schocken, 1949), which is divided into clear topics with lucid explanations and liberal quotations from the sources; and C. G. Montefiore and H. Loewe, *A Rabbinic Anthology* (New York: Meridian Books; and Philadelphia: Jewish Publication Society, 1960), which is the most ample collection and has critical, explanatory essays, but is slightly harder to follow than the other two volumes.

None of those three works are scientific studies of Rabbinic writings. One older attempt to critically evaluate the Rabbinic writings by a sympathetic non-Jewish scholar is G. F. Moore, *Judaism in the First Centuries of the Christian Era* (Cambridge, Mass.: Harvard University Press, 1950). For a later critical study, see E. E. Urbach, *The Sages* (Jerusalem: Magnes Press, 1975), which gives a broad sense of the Rabbinic writings, with copious footnotes. *The Rabbinic Mind* by Max Kadushin (New York: Bloch, 1965) is an attempt to classify Rabbinic concepts, couched, unfortunately, in very dense prose. *Worship and Ethics* by the same author (New York: Bloch, 1963) is more approachable.

An introduction to reading the Talmud itself, and to Talmudic logic, can be found in Moses Mielziner's *Introduction to the Talmud* (New York: Bloch, originally published 1902, revised 1986). In a different vein, *Back to the Sources* (New York: Summit Books, 1984), a series of essays on the primary texts of the Jewish tradition, edited by Barry W. Holtz, is a help in understanding what the core works of Judaism are about and how to read them.

Finally, reflecting new developments in Jewish scholarship on the Rabbis is Jacob Neusner's *From Politics to Piety* (Englewood Cliffs, N.J.: Prentice-Hall, 1973).

4. JEWISH PHILOSOPHY

The standard guide to Jewish philosophy remains Julius Guttman's *Philosophies of Judaism,* translated by David W. Silverman (New York: Holt, Rinehart and Winston, 1964). This can be supplemented by *History of Medieval Jewish Philosophy* by Isaac Husik

(Philadelphia: Jewish Publication Society, 1948) and Natan Rosen-streich's *Jewish Philosophy in Modern Times* (New York: Holt, Rine-hart and Winston, 1968). All three works, however, are somewhat academic in tone. Louis Jacobs, *A Jewish Theology* (New York: Behr-man House, 1973), covers theological subjects topically with deep learning and an engaging, easily understood style.

Popular books that concentrate on specific thinkers, including those mentioned in the present work, are: Eugene Borowitz, *Choices in Modern Jewish Thought* (New York: Behrman House, 1983); William E. Kaufman, *Contemporary Jewish Philosophies* (New York: Behrman House, 1976); S. H. Bergman, *Faith and Reason* (New York: Schocken, 1963); and Arthur Cohen, *The Natural and the Supernatural Jew* (New York: Behrman House, 1979). All of these books will give a good sense of what is happening in modern Jewish thought, and enable the reader to move into the primary sources.

For Heschel, it makes sense to begin with his marvelous evoca-tion of time, space, and holiness in the Jewish tradition, in his brief book *The Sabbath* (New York: Farrar, Straus and Young, 1951). From there the reader might want to read a major statement, *God in Search of Man* (New York: Farrar, Straus and Giroux, 1955). A good selection of Heschel's work with an explanatory essay is *Between God and Man,* edited by Fritz A. Rothschild (New York: The Free Press, 1965).

For Buber, it is probably best to begin with his *Tales of the Hasidim* (New York: Schocken, 1966), to see how inspiring and accessible Buber can be, and only then tackle the difficult *I and Thou.* Many of Buber's other works on the Bible and Jewish philos-ophy are far easier to understand than *I and Thou,* and each one is rich in insight. A standard introduction to Buber's work is *Martin Buber: The Life of Dialogue* (Chicago: University of Chicago Press, 1955) by Maurice Friedman.

Three modern thinkers who were not discussed at all in this book but are important to modern Jewish thought are: Buber's contem-porary Franz Rosenzweig, best approached by way of Nahum Glatzer's *Franz Rosenzweig: His Life and Thought* (New York: Schocken, 1983); Joseph Soloveitchik, an Orthodox scholar and philosopher, whose demanding but rewarding *Halakhic Man* is available in English, translated by Lawrence Kaplan (Philadelphia: Jewish Publication

Society, 1983); and Mordecai Kaplan, whose classic work *Judaism as a Civilization* (New York: Thomas Yosselof, 1957; originally published 1934) shook up an entire generation of Jewish thinkers, in very different ways.

Finally, the editors of *Commentary* magazine published *The Condition of Jewish Belief* (New York: Macmillan, 1966), a symposium that reflects the views of a wide variety of modern Jewish thinkers. All the respondents were asked the same questions concerning revelation, chosenness, and related topics.

5. EVIL

In light of the Holocaust, the question of evil has received an enormous amount of attention in our time. Perhaps the best place to begin is with the story. For that, Elie Wiesel's books must be read. Three important early works, *Night, Dawn,* and *The Accident,* are now available in one book, *The Night Trilogy* (New York: Farrar, Straus and Giroux, 1987). Along with Wiesel's, other survivor testimony, such as that of Primo Levi, is vital. Works on the history of the period are pouring forth from the presses, but they must be accompanied by the witness of those who were there.

Philosophical reflections on the Holocaust have taken many forms. Some of it has reflected the anguish of disbelief. Richard Rubenstein's *After Auschwitz* (New York: Bobbs-Merrill, 1966) remains a disturbing work. Eliezer Berkovits, an Orthodox scholar, wrote an equally moving book, *Faith After the Holocaust* (New York: K'tav, N.Y., 1973), in part a reply to Rubenstein, in which he tries to present the case for continued faith.

Other important statements include the work of Emil Fackenheim, *God's Presence in History* (New York: Harper and Row, 1972), among his other books, and Arthur Cohen's *The Tremendum* (New York: Crossroad, 1988). An attempt to grapple with the problem in a new way, espousing "predicate theology," is Harold Schulweis's rich, intricate *Evil and the Morality of God* (Cincinnati: Hebrew Union College Press, 1984).

The classical work on evil is the biblical book of Job. There is an enormous amount of commentary on the book itself, as well as various works on the question of evil that take Job as a starting point, as does Harold Kushner's popular and moving work *When Bad Things Happen to Good People* (New York: Avon, 1981). Job is one work whose relevance, sadly, has never abated, and it continues to speak with tremendous eloquence and force.

6. MYSTICISM

While this book does not really deal with mysticism, Jewish mysticism has been undergoing a revival of sorts, and it is full of suggestive ideas. The standard introductory work remains *Major Trends in Jewish Mysticism* by the master scholar Gershom Scholem (New York: Schocken, 1981). It is not an easy book, as we might expect of a work that opens up a world of ideas so foreign to our own. Equally exciting, and also demanding, is a new work challenging many of Scholem's premises (and incidentally demonstrating from another angle the intimacy of God to the Talmudic Rabbis), *Kabbalah: New Perspectives* by Moshe Idel (New Haven: Yale University Press, 1988).

For a more accessible introduction, to "build up" to the other works, one might try *The Mystic Quest* by David S. Ariel (Northvale, N.J.: Jason Aronson, 1988), a lucid introduction to Jewish mystical ideas. A more personal account, with some interesting portraits of mystics along the way, is *9½ Mystics* by Herbert Wiener (New York: Collier Macmillan, 1969). Two works that anthologize important texts are Gershom Scholem's *Zohar* (New York: Schocken, 1949), a small sampling from the central work of Jewish mysticism, and Lawrence Fine's *Safed Spirituality* (New York: Paulist Press, 1984), which examines the teachings of Judaism's most famous mystical community.

Finally, for all the topics listed above, and much more, the *Encyclopedia Judaica* is a treasure house of information and bibliographical help (Jerusalem: Keter, 1974).

7. TRANSLATIONS OF PRIMARY SOURCES

The fundamental source of Jewish tradition, after the Bible, is the Babylonian Talmud, which is available in an eighteen-volume translation from the Soncino Press (London, 1935–52), edited by I. Epstein. Although the Talmud cannot really be understood without instruction, the translation can be helpful to those who wish to dip a toe into what is aptly called "the sea of Talmud."

There are in fact two versions of the Talmud, the Babylonian and the Palestinian (also called the Jerusalem Talmud). The Palestinian proved far less important in Jewish history and thought, and only now is a translation being done, under the editorship of Jacob Neusner (Chicago Studies in the History of Judaism, 1982 and ongoing).

The foundation document of the Talmud is the Mishna, which is available in an old, somewhat unreliable, but helpfully annotated translation by H. Danby (London: Oxford University Press, 1933). A more accurate and lucid translation, with notes incorporated in the text, is *The Mishna*, edited by Jacob Neusner (New Haven: Yale University Press, 1988). One section of the Mishna has long been favored by writers and students. Pirke Avoth, variously translated as "Ethics of the Fathers," "Chapters of the Fathers," and "Wisdom of the Fathers," is a series of ethical maxims, and is available in many editions with many different commentaries.

The most extensive collection of Midrash in Rabbinic literature is *Midrash Rabbah*, which is available from Soncino Press (London, 1983) in ten volumes under the editorship of H. Freedman and Maurice Simon.

Various other collections of Rabbinic Midrash are available. To mention but a few, Pirke de Rabbi Eliezer was translated and annotated by Gerald Friedlander (New York: Sepher-Hermon Press, 1916). The Mechilta of Rabbi Ishmael is available in a translation by Jacob Lauterbach (Philadelphia: Jewish Publication Society, 1933). William Braude and Israel Kapstein have rendered Pesikta de-Rab Kahana as well as Tanna debe Eliyyahu (Seder Eliyahu Rabbah and Zuta) into English; both are available from the Jewish Publication Society of Philadelphia, 1975 and 1981 respectively. The same William Braude has, in the Yale University Judaica series, translated The Midrash on Psalms and Pesikta Rabbati, 1959 and 1968 respectively. With Rabbinic literature, even in translation, it is a great help to have a guide through the thicket of texts. As Pirke Avoth teaches, the best way to study is to find oneself a teacher, and learn together with a friend.

Finally in Midrash, a monument to scholarship is Louis Ginzburg's *The Legends of the Jews,* in seven volumes (Philadelphia: Jewish Publication Society, 1909–38), which is also available in a one-volume condensation. Ginzburg strung together thousands of Midrashim and forged a coherent, readable narrative. A glance at the two volumes of notes suggests the staggering erudition the enterprise required. Yet the story itself reads charmingly and gracefully.

Much more information and guidance are available than this brief list has been able to suggest. One book leads inevitably to another, and part of the pleasure of study is the enchantment of ending up in unexpected places.

Index